READY STEADY COOK 4

READY STEADY COOK 4

AINSLEY HARRIOTT

ROSS BURDEN

PHOTOGRAPHS BY
JULIET PIDDINGTON

BBC BOOKS

This book is published to accompany the television series *Ready Steady Cook*
which is produced by Bazal Productions Ltd for the BBC

Executive Producer: Linda Clifford
Producer: Mary Ramsay

Published by BBC Books, an imprint of BBC Worldwide Ltd,
Woodlands, 80 Wood Lane, London, W12 0TT

First published in 1997
Compiled by Bazal Productions Ltd
Recipes copyright © Ainsley Harriott and Ross Burden 1997
Photographs by Juliet Piddington, copyright © BBC Worldwide Publishing 1997
Home Economist: Sarah Ramsbottom

ISBN 0 563 38362 3

Designed by Louise Morley
Printed by Martins the Printers Ltd, Berwick-upon-Tweed
Bound by Hunter & Foulis Ltd, Edinburgh
Colour separation by Radstock Reproductions Ltd, Midsomer Norton
Colour printing by Lawrence Allen Ltd, Weston-super-Mare
Cover printed by Belmont Press Ltd, Northampton

CONTENTS

INTRODUCTION

Well, we've made over 300 programmes, survived two fires in one show and I've had half a pint of cream squirted in my face. It's been another fun-packed year on **Ready Steady Cook**. Doesn't time fly?

And as regular viewers of **Ready Steady Cook** must know by now, I am not the world's greatest cook, but I am always on hand to advise chefs on how to make instant mashed potato and the best thing to do with a gravy granule. Now they are things I know how to cook.

But I still do occasionally try and have a go at all the lovely recipes that our chefs rustle up on the programme and always keep my **Ready Steady Cook** recipe books on hand. And here's yet another delicious selection, this time from Ainsley and Ross, to give me a bit of incentive to get in the kitchen. I hope it works for you.

Happy cooking!

Presenter, **Ready Steady Cook**

A Note on Ingredients and Techniques

Good-quality ingredients make all the difference to the taste of the finished dish. For best results, choose unsalted butter and extra virgin olive oil. Buy ripe, flavoursome tomatoes, and whenever possible, really fresh herbs. If a recipe specifies dried herbs, freeze-dried ones usually have the best flavour. For desserts, chocolate should contain at least 50 per cent cocoa solids – check the back of the wrapper.

Some of the recipes contain raw or lightly cooked eggs. Because of the slight risk of salmonella poisoning, these should be avoided by the sick, the elderly, the very young, and pregnant women. The chances of contamination are greatly reduced if you buy free-range eggs, preferably organic, from a reputable supplier.

Many of the recipes in this book include wine. Use a wine that you would enjoy drinking rather than cheap 'cooking' wine – if it's not worth drinking it's not worth cooking with! You can use unsweetened apple juice or stock if you prefer.

The chefs on **Ready Steady Cook** often cook on a ridged grill pan. Ridged grill pans are made of cast iron and usually have a spout for pouring off the cooking juices. They are a very healthy way of cooking because the ridges keep the food raised above any fat that runs off. They also make attractive grill marks on food – to make a criss-cross pattern, give the food a half-turn halfway through cooking each side. Use ridged grill pans for steaks, chops, fish or chunky slices of vegetables such as aubergines, courgettes or peppers.

Finally, **Ready Steady Cook** is all about putting together a delicious meal from whatever ingredients you have to hand. The recipes in this book are proof that some of the most memorable dishes are the ones that come about on the spur of the moment. So, if you don't have a particular ingredient, follow the example of our chefs and improvise. Don't be afraid to get in the kitchen and **Ready Steady Cook!**

If you are trying to cut calories or reduce the fat in your diet it doesn't mean you have to miss out on taste or cooking these recipes. Check out some healthy alternatives. Buy trimmed or extra lean meat and bacon and remove the skin from chicken pieces. Use half-fat hard cheeses and semi-skimmed milk.
For everyday use, why not try low-fat fromage frais and low-fat natural yoghurt as substitutes for cream and crème fraiche.
Opt for low-fat soft cheese or quark instead of cream cheese.
Cook with sunflower, vegetable or olive oil in place of butter where possible.

LARDER INGREDIENTS USED ON
READY STEADY COOK

Arrowroot
Baking powder
Balsamic vinegar
Bay leaves
Beef stock cubes
Bottle of red wine
Bottle of white wine
Cardamom pods
Caster sugar
Cayenne pepper
Chicken stock cubes
Chilli powder
Clear honey
Cocoa powder
Cornflour
Demerara sugar
Dijon mustard
Double cream
Dried mixed herbs
Dried oregano
Eggs, size 3
Fresh basil
Fresh chervil

Fresh chives
Fresh coriander
Fresh dill
Fresh mint
Fresh parsley
Fresh rosemary
Fresh sage
Fresh thyme
Fresh white bread
Garam masala
Garlic
Golden syrup
Granulated sugar
Greek yoghurt
Ground all-spice
Ground cinnamon
Ground coriander
Ground cumin
Ground ginger
Ground nutmeg
Icing Sugar
Lemons/limes
Milk

Olive oil
Oranges
Paprika
Peppercorns
Plain flour
Red-wine vinegar
Salt
Self-raising flour
Sesame oil
Soft brown sugar
Soy sauce
Sunflower oil
Tabasco sauce
Tomato purée
Tomato sauce
Turmeric
Unsalted butter
Vegetable stock cubes
Vanilla essence
Vanilla pod
White-wine vinegar
Wholegrain mustard
Worcestershire sauce

VEGETARIAN DISHES

THE STAR OF CHRISTMAS – 10

SANDAL BURGERS – 12

NIGHTMARE ON PUMPKIN STREET – 14

GOOD ENOUGH TO GET OUT OF BED FOR – 15

NUREYEV'S HALLOWE'EN PUMPKIN AND GLAZED
TOFFEE APPLES – 17

ESCORT TERRACE RISOTTO WITH THREE
CHIMNEYS – 18

EDWARD'S MARVELLOUS MUSHROOMS – 19

FRANTIC BROCCOLI AND CHEESE SOUFFLÉS – 21

ROSS BURDEN

THE STAR OF CHRISTMAS

Star-shaped chestnut pastries, with stuffed mushrooms and creamy celery sauce

See photograph

Weight-Watchers lecturer, Maralyn Braybrook, asked Ross for a healthy meal for Christmas as she had to be seen to be good in case any of her 'pupils' were watching!

SERVES 4

450 g (1 lb) puff pastry
435 g (15¼ oz) can of chestnut purée
1 egg, beaten
225 g (8 oz) button mushrooms
4 tablespoons olive oil
1 onion, finely chopped
100 g (4 oz) Stilton cheese, crumbled
50 g (2 oz) walnut halves, roughly chopped

350 ml (12 fl oz) white wine
5 celery sticks, cut in 2.5 cm (1 inch) lengths
3 tablespoons double cream
2 tablespoons snipped fresh chives
25 g (1 oz) butter
Salt and freshly ground black pepper
Sprigs of flatleaf parsley, chives and celery leaves, to garnish

Pre-heat the oven to gas mark 7,220°C,425°F. Roll out half of the pastry on a lightly floured surface to a 25 cm (10 inch) square about 5 mm (¼ inch) thick and cut into four squares. Repeat with the other half of the pastry. Spoon 4 tablespoons of chestnut purée in the centre of one piece of pastry. Brush the edges of the pastry with beaten egg and cover with another piece of pastry. Press the edges together to seal well.

Place a bowl measuring about 11.5 cm (4½ inches) over the top and use as a guide to cut the pastry into a circle. Cut a zig-zag around the edge, to give a star shape. Score the top of the star from the centre to the zig-zag border, at 1 cm (½ inch) intervals. Brush with more beaten egg and put on a greased baking sheet. Repeat, to make four stars. Bake for 12–15 minutes, until the pastry is well risen and golden.

Remove the stalks from the mushrooms and make a hollow in each cap. Chop the stalks roughly. Heat 2 tablespoons of oil in a pan, add the onion and cook for 3 minutes, stirring occasionally. Add the mushroom stalks and cook for 2 minutes. Stir in the Stilton and walnuts and season with pepper. Spoon the mixture into the mushroom caps. Heat the other 2 tablespoons of oil in a frying-pan, add the filled mushrooms and cook for 3 minutes. Pour 150 ml (5 fl oz) of wine into the pan, cover and cook gently for 8 minutes.

Put the celery, remaining wine and some salt and pepper in a pan and simmer for 8–10 minutes, until softened. Put in a food processor, with the cream, and process until smooth. Push through a sieve back into the pan, add the chives and butter and heat until the butter has melted.

To serve, put the chestnut stars on a serving plate and place the filled mushrooms, with their cooking juices, to one side. Spoon the celery sauce around the edge of the chestnut stars and garnish with sprigs of flatleaf parsley, chives and celery leaves.

READY STEADY COOK Tips
Steamed spinach and ricotta cheese could be used in place of chestnut purée.

Parsley is the most widely used herb and there are now two kinds available. Flatleaf parsley is regarded as less bitter and has a fuller flavour than the more common curly parsley. Flatleaf is great in salads, but can be interchanged with curly in almost any savoury dish. Don't throw away the stalks; their concentrated flavour is ideal for use in a bouqet garni to flavour stock, soups and casseroles.

ROSS BURDEN

SANDAL BURGERS

Sheila Lawson had been vegetarian for 8 years but had always avoided tofu as she had absolutely no idea what to do with it. 'It never looks very appetizing!' she said. Ross managed, of course, to change her mind.

SERVES 2
FOR THE SAUCE
1 red pepper, quartered and seeded
6 tablespoons olive oil
1 tablespoon white-wine vinegar

FOR THE BURGERS
50 g (2 oz) cashew nuts
225 g (8 oz) smoked tofu
1 garlic clove, crushed
2 eggs
Handful of fresh coriander leaves
1 teaspoon soy sauce

1 tablespoon sunflower oil
Sprigs of chervil or parsley, to garnish

FOR THE STIR-FRY
100 g (4 oz) long-grain rice
200 g (7 oz) mixed baby corn and mangetout
2 tablespoons sesame oil
3 spring onions, chopped
3 tablespoons snipped fresh chives
3 tablespoons soy sauce
Salt and freshly ground black pepper
Fresh chervil and coriander, to garnish

Pre-heat the oven to gas mark 7, 220°C, 425°F. Cook the rice for the stir-fry in salted, boiling water for 10–12 minutes, until tender. Drain and reserve. Put the pepper on a baking tray and roast for about 10 minutes. Put in a plastic bag until cool enough to handle.

Toast the cashew nuts in a dry frying-pan over a high heat, until golden brown, shaking continuously. In a food processor, process the tofu, garlic and cashew nuts roughly and then add the eggs, coriander leaves and soy sauce. Process again, to form a thick mixture. Flour your hands well and shape the mixture into four burgers. Heat the sunflower oil in a frying-pan and cook the burgers for 2 minutes on each side.

Remove the skin from the roast red pepper. Put the flesh into the clean processor bowl, together with the olive oil and vinegar, and process until smooth.

Slice the baby corn and mangetout diagonally into chunks and cook in salted, boiling water for 3 minutes. Drain. Heat the sesame oil in a wok and add the spring onions, baby corn and mangetout; cook for 1–2 minutes and then add the rice, chives and soy sauce. Season. Stir-fry for 3–4 minutes, until heated through.

To serve, drizzle the pepper sauce round the outside of the plate, pile the tofu burgers in the centre and garnish with sprigs of chervil or parsley. Serve the rice in a bowl, garnished with coriander and chervil leaves.

READY STEADY COOK Tips

You could grill the peppers under a hot grill for 10–12 minutes, instead of roasting them, to avoid heating the oven. Alternatively, hold the pepper over a gas flame on a skewer, until the skin is blackened.

Put the roasted/grilled pepper in a plastic bag or in a bowl covered with cling film and leave for a few minutes. The skin will come away easily.

ROSS BURDEN

NIGHTMARE ON PUMPKIN STREET

Pumpkin ravioli with sage butter sauce

Our Hallowe'en contestant, Amanda Ward-Baker, told Fern she was bullied to come on the show by her daughters Ebony-Rose and Ella – our number one fans. Spookily, even their goldfish are called Ainsley and Lesley!

SERVES 2	1 egg yolk
FOR THE PASTA	1 egg, lightly beaten
225 g (8 oz) plain flour	Salt
2 eggs	
Salt	**FOR THE SAUCE**
FOR THE FILLING	100 g (4 oz) butter
1 tablespoon mixed candied peel	2 tablespoons chopped fresh sage
50 g (2 oz) flaked almonds	Grated nutmeg
250 g (9 oz) ricotta	1 tablespoon freshly grated Parmesan, to serve
¼ pumpkin, peeled, seeded and chopped	Fresh sage leaves, to garnish

To make the pasta, put the flour, eggs and a pinch of salt in a food processor and process until the mixture resembles breadcrumbs. Put the mixture on to the work surface and work it together. Lightly knead, cover with cling film and leave to one side to rest.

Meanwhile, in a food processor, process the mixed peel and almonds for 10 seconds. Add the ricotta, pumpkin flesh and egg yolk and process until smooth.

Divide the pasta dough into four. Roll out each piece thinly to a rectangle about 25 cm x 20 cm (10 inches x 8 inches), using either a pasta machine or a rolling pin. Lay the pasta on the floured work surface and put 2 teaspoons of the pumpkin mixture in an even row on two of the sheets. Brush round the filling with the beaten egg. Place the other two sheets on top and press round each mound of filling, to seal well. Using a 5 cm (2 inch) pastry cutter, cut round each mound. Bring a pan of salted water to the boil and cook the pasta for 3 minutes.

Meanwhile, melt the butter in a small pan and, when bubbling, add the sage and season with nutmeg. Drain the pasta and put on to a serving plate. Pour over the butter sauce. Sprinkle over the Parmesan and garnish with sage leaves.

READY STEADY COOK Tips

Make sure the ravioli are well sealed before cooking or they will come apart in the water.

Parmigiano Reggiano is the very best Parmesan you can buy. Grate it or, if you prefer, shave it with a vegetable peeler and scatter over pasta, salads and vegetables. Grano Padano is almost as good but not quite as tasty. Store your chunk of Parmesan in the fridge or freezer, wrapped in foil.

R O S S　 B U R D E N

GOOD ENOUGH TO GET OUT OF BED FOR

Deep-fried aubergine slices with feta filling, filo money bags and two pepper relishes

Julia Walker confessed to Ross that she is incredibly lazy in the kitchen. She can never be bothered to cook, and has had a washing machine for over a year and still doesn't know how to use it. Ross thought this was just the thing to ease her in gently.

SERVES 2	1 yellow pepper, seeded and quartered
½ aubergine, thinly sliced	3 tablespoons olive oil
1 red pepper, seeded and quartered	75 g (3 oz) butter

½ onion, thinly sliced
1 tablespoon balsamic vinegar
2 teaspoons brown sugar
1 sheet fresh filo pastry
6 fresh chives
1 courgette
Juice of 1 lemon

Oil, for deep-frying
200 g (7 oz) feta
3 tablespoons Greek yoghurt
1 tablespoon chopped fresh basil
2 tomatoes, skinned, seeded and diced
Salt and freshly ground black pepper

Pre-heat the oven to gas mark 7, 220°C, 425°F. Put the aubergine slices in a colander, sprinkle with salt and leave to drain, to extract the bitter juices.

Put the pepper quarters on a baking sheet and roast until the skins blacken. Then put them in a bowl, cover with cling film and leave for 3–5 minutes. Take the skins off and blend the yellow pepper with a tablespoon of olive oil in a processor, until smooth. Transfer to a bowl. Do the same with the red pepper. Keep to one side.

Heat 25 g (1 oz) of butter in a small pan and gently fry the onion until softened. Stir in the vinegar and sugar and caramelize. Keep to one side. Melt the rest of the butter. Cut the sheet of filo into six squares. Grease a baking sheet with some of the melted butter and put the filo squares on the sheet. Place a teaspoon of onion mixture in the centre of each square and draw each corner together to create a 'money bag'. Tie each with a chive. Brush the money bags with more melted butter and cook in the oven for 4 minutes, or until the pastry is golden.

Cut the courgette into long, thin strips and put them in a large mixing bowl. Pour on the last tablespoon of olive oil and the lemon juice. Season. Put a smaller bowl inside, to press down the courgette.

Meanwhile, heat a deep pan with the oil. Rinse the aubergine slices and drain them well on kitchen paper. Deep-fry for 2–3 minutes, until golden and crisp.

Put the feta, Greek yoghurt and basil in a blender and process until smooth.

In the centre of the plate, layer the aubergine and the feta mixture. Arrange the filo parcels around the plate. Spoon on the pepper relishes and scatter on the courgette and tomato pieces.

NUREYEV'S HALLOWE'EN PUMPKIN AND GLAZED TOFFEE APPLES

Vegetable curry served in a pumpkin, with caramelized apple rings and yoghurt

Georgina Ward does all the cooking at home because 'it gives me time by myself – I can get away from baby and husband and shut myself in the kitchen with a glass of red wine, Prokofiev and oodles of garlic.'

SERVES 4
FOR THE PUMPKIN
1.5 kg (3 lb) pumpkin
350 g (12 oz) potatoes, cut in 2 cm (¾ inch) cubes
2 tablespoons olive oil
1 onion, chopped
1 garlic clove, finely chopped
8 cardamom pods
2 teaspoons curry powder
Pinch of ground cloves
225 g (8 oz) tomatoes, cut into wedges

1 tablespoon chopped fresh coriander
Salt and freshly ground black pepper
Sprigs of fresh coriander, to garnish

FOR THE TOFFEE APPLES
4 dessert apples, cored and cut in 1 cm (½ inch) rings
Juice of 1 lemon
4 tablespoons icing sugar
½ teaspoon ground cinnamon
225 g (8 oz) Greek yoghurt

Pre-heat the oven to gas mark 6, 200°C, 400°F. Make zig-zag cuts around the top of the pumpkin and lift off the 'lid'. Scoop out and discard the seeds and then carefully cut out the pumpkin flesh, to leave a 1 cm (½ in) thick shell. Put the pumpkin shell in the oven for 10–15 minutes, until the skin is slightly charred.

Cut the pumpkin flesh into 2 cm (¾ inch) cubes. Cook the pumpkin and potato in boiling water for 6–8 minutes, until almost tender.

17

Heat the oil in a frying-pan, add the onion, garlic, cardamom pods, curry powder and ground cloves, season with salt and pepper and cook for 4 minutes, stirring occasionally. Drain the pumpkin and potatoes and add to the frying-pan, with the tomatoes and coriander. Season with salt and pepper. Cook for a further 5 minutes, stirring occasionally. Spoon the vegetable curry into the pumpkin shell and garnish with sprigs of coriander.

Put the apple rings on a baking tray and sprinkle over the lemon juice and icing sugar. Put under a hot grill for 5–8 minutes, until the apple rings have caramelized. Sprinkle the cinnamon over the yoghurt and serve with the glazed toffee apples.

AINSLEY HARRIOTT

ESCORT TERRACE RISOTTO WITH THREE CHIMNEYS

Student Liz lives with 5 other girls and they each take turns in cooking. Liz's day is Wednesday and she wanted something to impress them with so Ainsley came up with this gorgeous mushroom and cheese risotto.

SERVES 4	1 tablespoon chopped fresh coriander
2 tablespoons olive oil	450 ml (1 pint) vegetable stock
1 onion, chopped	300 g (11 oz) can of garden peas, drained
225 g (8 oz) mushrooms, sliced	6 pick and mix cheeses (2 Boursin, 2 Danish
(keep 3 large ones whole)	blue and 2 Bel Paese), cubed
225 g (8 oz) long-grain white rice	Salt and freshly ground black pepper
150 ml (5 fl oz) white wine	1 lemon and 1 lime, sliced, to garnish (optional)
1 teaspoon ground cumin	Leaves of fresh coriander, to garnish

In a large pan, heat the oil and cook the onion for 3 minutes, until softened. Stir in the sliced mushrooms and cook for a further 2 minutes.

Add the rice, wine, cumin and chopped coriander. Slowly add the stock, stirring occasionally, and cook for 10 minutes, until the rice swells and is tender. Add the peas, cover and cook for a further 5 minutes. Stir in half of the chopped Boursin and Danish blue for the last minute of the cooking time. Pre-heat the grill to hot.

Slice off the stalks of the three whole mushrooms and stuff with the Bel Paese cheese. Place on the grill pan. Shake a little olive oil on to each mushroom, season and grill for 8–10 minutes, until the cheese is melted and the mushrooms have browned.

To serve, put the risotto on a large plate, sprinkle the rest of the cheese over the rice and place the stuffed mushrooms on top.

Garnish with a few leaves of coriander, and slices of lemon and lime, if you like.

A I N S L E Y   H A R R I O T T

EDWARD'S MARVELLOUS MUSHROOMS

Mushrooms stuffed with leek, cheese and nut soufflé, with leek and mushroom lasagne

Student Edward Warren told Ainsley that *Ready Steady Cook* was a cult show in his house. He wanted to cook something a bit posh for his fellow housemates for under a fiver.

SERVES 2	200 ml (7 fl oz) crème fraîche
4 large mushrooms	2 eggs, separated
2 tablespoons olive oil	1½ tablespoons vegetarian Cheddar, grated
100 g (4 oz) walnut pieces	2 tablespoons olive oil
1 leek, sliced	4 small mushrooms, chopped
150 ml (5 fl oz) white wine	4 fresh lasagne sheets
25 g (1 oz) butter	Salt and freshly ground black pepper
50 g (2 oz) plain flour	

Pre-heat the oven to gas mark 7, 220°C, 425°F. Wipe the large mushrooms and remove and discard the stalks. Put the mushrooms on to a baking sheet and drizzle over 1 tablespoon of olive oil. Season and bake for 5 minutes.

Meanwhile, dry-fry the walnuts, until browned, turning occasionally. Heat the remaining tablespoon of olive oil in a pan and sauté the leek for 4 minutes, until softened. Then add 30 ml (1 fl oz) of white wine.

To make the soufflé, melt the butter in a pan. Stir in the flour. Stir in half the crème fraiche and, when thickened, beat in the egg yolks. Whisk the egg whites until stiff. Put half the egg yolk mixture in a bowl. Stir in half the leek, the cheese and 2 tablespoons of the nuts and season. Fold in the egg whites. Put a few nuts on each mushroom. Spoon on the soufflé and bake for 5–6 minutes until golden and risen. Add the remaining crème fraiche and 90 ml (3 fl oz) of white wine to the remaining egg yolk mixture and warm through in a small pan.

Heat a tablespoon of oil in a pan and sauté the chopped mushrooms. Add the remaining leek, remaining 30 ml (1 fl oz) of white wine and any remaining nuts.

Bring a pan of salted water to the boil and cook the lasagne sheets for 1 minute. Drain. Cut each sheet in half.

Put two lasagne strips on each plate. Spoon on the sautéd leeks and the mushrooms and then add a layer of pasta. Spoon on the sauce and drizzle over the remaining tablespoon of olive oil. Serve the soufflés separately.

READY STEADY COOK Tip

If you are feeling really extravagant, use fresh wild mushrooms in place of chopped mushrooms. Packs are available in most large supermarkets and it beats putting on your wellies and going armed with a reference book to gather them yourself.

A I N S L E Y   H A R R I O T T

FRANTIC BROCCOLI AND CHEESE SOUFFLÉS

Broccoli and cheese soufflés, with mushroom croutes
and hollandaise sauce.
See photograph

Annette Pyke told us that she loves cooking but it's wasted at home because husband Steven
'eats like a child – even at Christmas he had sausage and chips instead of turkey.' She added,
'It's like feeding a third child, although the kids' tastes have got sophisticated.'

SERVES 3

FOR THE SOUFFLÉS
2 tablespoons olive oil
4 tablespoons grated Parmesan
275 ml (9 fl oz) milk
25 g (1 oz) butter
25 g (1 oz) plain flour
¼ teaspoon grated nutmeg
225 g (8 oz) broccoli, green florets only, cut
into small pieces
150 g (5 oz) Gruyère cheese, grated
3 eggs, separated
Salt and freshly ground black pepper

FOR THE CROUTES
25 g (1 oz) butter
225 g (8 oz) button mushrooms, sliced
75 ml (3 fl oz) double cream
1 tablespoon finely chopped fresh parsley
3–4 tablespoons olive oil
6 slices of French bread, cut on the diagonal

FOR THE SAUCE
2 tablespoons white-wine vinegar
10 peppercorns
3 egg yolks
175 g (6 oz) unsalted butter, melted
Salt and freshly ground black pepper

Pre-heat the oven to gas mark 4, 180°C, 350°F. Brush the insides of
six 150 ml (5 fl oz) ramekins with a little oil and coat with 3 tablespoons
of the Parmesan cheese. Heat the milk in a pan, until almost simmering.
  Heat the butter in a pan and, when bubbling, add the flour and
cook for a minute, stirring constantly. Pour in the hot milk and whisk

over a medium heat, until the mixture is smooth and simmering. Remove from the heat and season with grated nutmeg, salt and pepper.

Cook the broccoli for 5–6 minutes until tender, drain and mash just enough to give small pieces. Stir the broccoli, Gruyère and egg yolks into the sauce.

Whisk the egg whites until they form soft peaks and gently fold into the broccoli mixture. Divide between the six ramekins, sprinkle over the remaining tablespoon of grated Parmesan and bake in the oven for 15 minutes, until risen and golden.

For the croutes, heat 25 g (1 oz) of the butter in a pan and sauté the mushrooms for 5 minutes. Season well and stir in the double cream and parsley. Keep warm until ready to serve. In a separate frying-pan, heat 3–4 tablespoons of olive oil and sauté the bread slices, until golden on each side.

To make the hollandaise sauce, heat the white-wine vinegar in a small pan, with 3 tablespoons of water and the peppercorns. Reduce this mixture to a tablespoon and pour into a food processor bowl. Add to this 3 egg yolks. Pour the melted butter slowly into the egg yolk and vinegar mixture, while the processor is running. Process until the sauce is thickened and then season to taste.

To serve, place the bread slices on a plate, top with the mushrooms and pour over the hollandaise sauce. Serve the soufflés to one side.

READY STEADY COOK Tip
When folding the egg whites into the broccoli mixture, add a tablespoon, then stir in well to loosen the mixture slightly. Fold in the remaining egg whites with a large metal tablespoon, in a figure of eight, being careful not to knock out too much air.

FISH AND SHELLFISH

LASAGNE FRUTTI DI MARE – 24

BRUSCHETTA PESCE – 26

ZUPPA ALLA VONGOLE (CLAM SOUP) – 28

NINA'S SEAFOOD – 29

CRESPELLINE AMAZING GRACE – 31

HOKI POACHI JOSEPHINE – 33

ROCK OKRA AND FISH CAKES, WITH A
COCONUT MALAYSIAN-DAWN SAUCE – 34

SWEET CAROLINE'S CALAMITY MACKEREL – 36

FIERY-FARING SALMON – 37

A LOAD OF OLD SCALLOPS – 38

ROSS BURDEN

LASAGNE FRUTTI DI MARE

Lasagne with seafood in tomato sauce, with avocado sauce and
courgette ribbons
See photograph

Sheila Davies had two favourite dishes – pasta and seafood.
Ross wanted to make her the perfect combination and came up
with this deliciously simple dish.

SERVES 3–4	2 tablespoons chopped fresh basil
5 tomatoes	1 avocado
1 courgette	10 g (½ oz) butter
Juice of 1 lemon	1 tablespoon lime juice
5 tablespoons olive oil	2 tablespoons crème fraiche
1 red onion, chopped	1 tablespoon balsamic vinegar
2 garlic cloves, thinly sliced	Salt and freshly ground black pepper
250 g (9 oz) fresh lasagne sheets	
200 g (7 oz) tub pre-cooked mixed seafood	
(sliced squid, mussels, prawns)	

Score the tomatoes and plunge in boiling water for 1 minute. Drain
and, when cool enough to handle, remove the skins. Cut into quarters
and scoop out the seeds into a sieve placed over a bowl, to catch the
juices. Roughly chop the tomato flesh and set aside.

Top and tail the courgette and then use a potato peeler to slice thinly
lengthways into a large bowl. Add the lemon juice and 2 tablespoons
of olive oil. Season and stir, to coat the courgette. Place a smaller
bowl on top of the courgette slices and fill it with cold water. Leave for
5 minutes; the lemon juice will gently cook the courgette.

Meanwhile, heat a tablespoon of olive oil in a pan over a gentle
heat and add the onion and garlic. Season with pepper and sauté for

5 minutes, until the onion has softened. Set aside to cool.

Cut circles from the lasagne sheets, using a pastry cutter. Bring a pan of salted water to the boil and add a dash of olive oil. Add the pasta and cook for 2–3 minutes, until *al dente*. Drain when cooked.

Meanwhile, add the tomato flesh and reserved juice to the cooled onions and garlic, with a further tablespoon of olive oil. Leave to cook very gently for 5 minutes. Rinse the seafood under running water, drain and add to the pan, with the chopped basil, to heat through for 3 minutes.

Halve the avocado, remove the stone and scoop out the flesh with a large, round spoon. Roughly chop the flesh. Heat the butter in a small pan over a gentle heat and sauté the avocado flesh for a minute on each side, seasoning with pepper. Add the lime juice and crème fraiche and gently shake the pan, to mix.

To serve, put a circle of lasagne on each plate. Layer up lasagne, seafood in tomato sauce and avocado, finishing with pasta. Top with the courgette ribbons and drizzle the plate with the remaining tablespoon of olive oil and the balsamic vinegar.

READY STEADY COOK Tip
Serve this with crusty bread, as there are lots of delicious juices to soak up.

BRUSCHETTA PESCE

Toasted bread topped with red pepper, with sardines
and artichoke

Janette Tovey told us that her husband's favourite hobby was fishing, but if he ever caught anything big enough, she always had problems gutting and preparing the fish. Ross came up with this lovely sardine dish, which shouldn't create too many problems for her.

SERVES 2
Juice of 1 lemon
1 globe artichoke
1 bunch of spring onions
1 red pepper, seeded and quartered
4 slices of bread from a country loaf
1 garlic clove
Olive oil
4 fresh sardines
Seasoned flour, for coating

FOR THE MAYONNAISE
Salt and freshly ground black pepper
2 egg yolks
1 teaspoon caster sugar
1 teaspoon Dijon mustard
2 teaspoons white-wine vinegar
250 ml (9 fl oz) sunflower oil

TO SERVE
1 tablespoon balsamic vinegar
Chervil sprigs, to garnish
Grated zest of 1 lemon

Pre-heat the oven to gas mark 7, 220°C, 425°F. Bring a small pan of water to the boil and add half the lemon juice. To prepare the artichoke bottom, cut or break off the stalk. Using a very sharp knife, carefully cut round the whole artichoke to remove all the outside leaves and discard them. This will leave a cone shape of soft leaves. Trim off any remaining green parts. Cut or snap off the top of the cone and discard, to leave you just the choke bottom. This contains a hairy, inedible centre that is much easier to remove after cooking. Place the artichoke bottom into the boiling water and lemon juice and cook for 8 minutes, or until tender when pierced with a knife, then drain. Leave to cool slightly, then scoop out the inedible centre with a teaspoon and cut the artichoke bottom into quarters.

Cut the green tails off the spring onions and, leaving one end intact, cut into long strips. Put into a bowl of cold water and leave to one side.

Meanwhile, put the pepper quarters on a baking sheet and bake until the skin is blackened.

Heat a griddle pan. Griddle the bread on one side and then turn over. Rub with garlic and drizzle on some olive oil. Remove from the pan.

Heat some olive oil in a large deep frying-pan. To prepare the sardines, cut off the heads and remove the innards. Press them, flesh-side down, on to a board; this will enable the tail and bones to come out in one. Lightly coat the sardines in the flour and fry in the pan for about 2–3 minutes on each side; drain on kitchen paper.

Meanwhile, make the mayonnaise by whisking the egg yolks with a pinch of salt. Add the caster sugar, mustard, vinegar and remaining lemon juice and, whilst continuing to whisk, gradually add the sunflower oil. Season with salt and pepper.

When the skin of the pepper is blackened, leave to steam in a bowl covered with cling film for a couple of minutes. Peel off the skin when it is cool enough to handle.

Arrange the slices of bruschetta, with the red pepper and the artichoke on each plate. Put the sardines on each plate and spoon some of the mayonnaise on to the artichoke. Drizzle some more olive oil and the balsamic vinegar over the peppers and garnish with chervil, lemon zest and the spring-onion tails.

READY STEADY COOK Tip
If you don't fancy preparing globe artichokes, you can buy canned artichoke hearts, which are the pale, tender group of leaves taken from the middle of young artichokes that have not developed hairy, inedible chokes.

ROSS BURDEN

ZUPPA ALLA VONGOLE (CLAM SOUP)

Clams with spaghetti and tomato soup, with sage butter sauce

Coming from a large family, Ena Short was used to cooking in large quantities. Unfortunately, the first meal she cooked for her husband was so huge, the kitchen table collapsed! Ross's substantial soup should keep them all happy.

SERVES 2	1 fennel bulb, cut into small pieces
8 spring onions	1 tablespoon chopped fresh sage
4 tablespoons olive oil	225 g (8 oz) fresh spaghetti
400 g (14 oz) can of chopped tomatoes, drained	290 g (10½ oz) can of clams, drained
1 teaspoon ground turmeric	Salt and freshly ground black pepper
50 g (2 oz) butter	Fresh chives, chervil and basil leaves, to garnish
250 g (9 oz) broccoli, cut into small florets	

Cut the green ends off the spring onions and slice them thinly lengthways. Put into a bowl of cold water and keep to one side. Slice the rest of the spring onions finely. Heat 2 tablespoons of olive oil in a pan and gently fry the spring onions for 2–3 minutes, stirring occasionally, until soft. Then sieve the tomatoes into the pan. Add 150 ml (5 fl oz) of water. Stir and bring to the boil. Add the turmeric and 25 g (1 oz) of butter. Blend with a hand blender, until smooth. Season and keep warm.

Heat 2 tablespoons of olive oil in a shallow pan and fry the broccoli and fennel for 1–2 minutes. Season and drain on kitchen paper. Meanwhile, heat 25 g (1 oz) of butter in a frying-pan and fry the sage for 1 minute until crisp. Bring a pan of salted water to the boil and cook the spaghetti for 3–4 minutes. Drain.

Toss the spaghetti in the sage butter and, using a carving fork or similar, wind a skein of spaghetti and place it in the centre of a soup plate. Arrange the clams and fried vegetables around the pasta and pour the soup over the top. The clams will warm through in the soup. Garnish with the green ends of the spring onions, chives, chervil and basil.

READY STEADY COOK Tip
Spring onion tails go curly when left in cold water, and make a great garnish.

ROSS BURDEN

NINA'S SEAFOOD

Haddock and mussels, with watercress sauce, Parisienne potatoes and carrot ribbons
See photograph

Canadian Nina Cubrilo told Fern that she'd been in England for a while and was loving it, but there was just one problem. She said that unless she learned to cook at least one dish soon, she would starve to death! Ross thought this colourful seafood dish was a good one to start with.

SERVES 2

FOR THE SAUCE
1 tablespoon olive oil
1 onion, finely chopped
75 g (3 oz) watercress
4 tablespoons white wine
200 ml (7 fl oz) tub of crème fraiche
50 g (2 oz) butter, chilled and diced

FOR THE POTATOES
2 medium potatoes
Vegetable oil, for deep-frying
Salt and freshly ground black pepper

FOR THE FISH
1 haddock fillet
1 tablespoon olive oil
25 g (1 oz) butter
Plain flour, seasoned

FOR THE MUSSELS
4 tablespoons white wine
175 g (6 oz) live mussels
4 carrots
2 tablespoons olive oil
Salt and freshly ground black pepper

Heat the oil in a pan and cook the onion for 4 minutes, until softened. Add the watercress and cook for 3 minutes, until wilted. Add the wine and bring to the boil for a few seconds, then add the crème fraiche and cook for a further two minutes. Put into a food processor and process until smooth. Pass through a sieve into a clean pan and heat through. Just before serving, whisk in the butter, until thick and shiny.

Hollow out the potatoes with a melon baller. Heat the vegetable oil in a pan and fry the potato balls, until golden, crisp and soft in the centre. Drain on kitchen paper. Season.

Score the skin of the haddock. Heat the oil and butter in a frying-pan. Dip the fish in the seasoned flour and fry it skin-side down first for 7–10 minutes, until the skin is crisp and the flesh flakes when tested with a fork. Keep warm.

Heat the wine in a pan and add the mussels. Cover and cook until they open. Discard any of these that do not open. Peel the carrots and cut them into thin ribbons with a potato peeler or mandolin. Heat the olive oil in a pan and cook the carrot ribbons until softened. Season.

Spoon the carrots on to the plate and place the haddock on top. Arrange the mussels on the plate and pour the sauce around. Serve the potatoes separately.

READY STEADY COOK Tip
You could use a deep-fat fryer to fry the potato balls. Fry them for 4 minutes at 190°C/375°F.

CRESPELLINE AMAZING GRACE

Spinach and prawn pancakes, with piquant sauce and spinach salad

When Fern asked Guide leader Grace Essex why she brought raw prawns along, Grace said that she never normally bought them – because they looked so disgusting! Ross rose to the challenge and cooked up this beautiful dish for her.

SERVES 3–4

FOR THE SPINACH AND PRAWN PANCAKES
250 g (9 oz) spinach, washed
Olive oil for frying
100 g (4 oz) plain flour
Pinch of salt
1 egg
300 ml (10 fl oz) milk
2 tablespoons olive oil
15 g (½ oz) butter
250 g (9 oz) king prawns, peeled and de-veined
150 g (5 oz) goats' cheese
150 ml (5 fl oz) double cream
Salt and freshly ground black pepper

FOR THE COUNTRY SAUCE
1 onion, chopped
Olive oil for frying
2 carrots, grated
Tabasco sauce
2 tablespoons tomato purée
300 ml (10 fl oz) red wine

FOR THE SALAD
1 thin slice of bread, cubed
Olive oil for frying
1 tablespoon white-wine vinegar
4 tablespoons olive oil
Salt and freshly ground black pepper

Pre-heat the oven to gas mark 7, 220°C, 425°F. To make the spinach and prawn pancakes, remove the spinach stalks. Heat a pan with a little olive oil and quickly wilt half the spinach leaves. Mix the flour and salt together and then stir in the egg and milk. Heat the pancake pan with the olive oil and butter. Purée the spinach in a food processor and then mix into the pancake mixture.

Cook the pancakes until golden brown on each side. The mixture should make about 8 pancakes. Cook the prawns until pink on both sides in a small pan with a little olive oil. Remove from the pan and reserve. Season with salt and freshly ground black pepper.

To make the sauce, sauté the onion in a little olive oil for 3 minutes, until soft, using the pan that the prawns were fried in. Add the carrots and cook for 3–4 minutes, until softened. Add a dash of Tabasco sauce, the tomato purée and the red wine, and continue to cook.

Cut up 100 g (4 oz) of the cheese and blend it in a food processor, with the cream. Place a tablespoonful of the mix on the middle of a pancake, with a prawn. Fold into triangles. Repeat with the other pancakes. Arrange the triangles with the point up and the sealed side down in a large ovenproof baking dish. Top with the country sauce and bake for 12 minutes.

Place the remaining spinach leaves in a salad bowl. Fry the bread cubes in a little olive oil until golden and crisp. Make a vinaigrette with the white-wine vinegar and olive oil and season with salt and freshly ground black pepper. Mix in the remaining goats' cheese to a creamy consistency. Dress the salad and sprinkle with the croutons. Serve with the spinach and prawn pancakes and sauce.

READY STEADY COOK Tip
You could add a couple of sticks of celery to the country sauce. String the celery first then slice it into thin slivers and add it with the tomato purée.

Above: Lisa's Lazy Lamb and Lentil Curry (page 75).
Below: Boerewors Braii (page 61).

Above: The Cajun Gloucestershire Old Spot Chop (page 78).
Below: Pork Diane (page 65).

AINSLEY HARRIOTT

HOKI POACHI JOSEPHINE

Hoki roulade stuffed with carrot and leek, with pink fir apple potatoes and fennel sauce

Josie Anderson brought fish along in memory of the most disgusting meal she'd ever had – fish pie cooked by her daughter at school. Ainsley showed her how to cook hoki, which is similar to cod, in the hope that she'd pass on the recipe to her daughter.

SERVES 2	350 g (12 oz) hoki fillet
500 g (1 lb 2 oz) pink fir apple potatoes	1 small fennel bulb, chopped
2 carrots	40 g (1½ oz) butter
1 leek	2 tablespoons double cream
1 tablespoon olive oil	Salt and freshly ground black pepper
150 ml (5 fl oz) white wine	Fresh chives, to garnish
1 tablespoon chopped fresh dill	

Pre-heat the oven to gas mark 7, 220°C, 425°F. Scrub the potatoes and cook whole in boiling, salted water for 10–12 minutes, or until done. Drain, cut into thick slices and keep warm.

Prepare the carrots and leek and cut into matchsticks. Heat the oil and sauté the vegetables for about 3 minutes, to soften. Add 2 tablespoons of the wine, the dill and a little salt and pepper.

Skin the fish fillet and lay it, skinned-side up, on a board. Spread over the vegetables and roll up. Place the fish in a small, ovenproof dish, season and pour over all but 2 tablespoons of the remaining wine. Cover loosely and bake for 15–20 minutes, until the fish is cooked and the flesh flakes easily.

Meanwhile, sauté the fennel in the butter for 2–3 minutes, to soften. Add the 2 tablespoons of wine, the cream and a little seasoning and cook for a further 4–5 minutes, stirring occasionally. Purée the mixture in a blender or food processor, to give a smooth sauce, adding the fish cooking liquor as necessary, to give a pouring consistency. Return to the pan to re-heat; season to taste.

To serve, arrange the sliced potatoes around a hot serving plate and place the fish on top. Pour over the sauce and garnish with the chives, cut into 4 cm (1½ inch) lengths.

AINSLEY HARRIOTT

ROCK OKRA AND FISH CAKES, WITH A COCONUT MALAYSIAN-DAWN SAUCE

White fish cakes with coconut sauce and Thai-spiced okra
See photograph

Dawn Gregory loves cooking, and, together with her two sons,
sings along at the same time using carrots as microphones. Ainsley thought up this delicate,
spicy dish to delight them all.

SERVES 2

FOR THE FISH CAKES
450 g (1 lb) haddock or cod, very finely chopped
2 tablespoons chopped fresh dill
150 g (5 oz) plain flour
1 large egg, beaten
Salt and freshly ground black pepper
3 tablespoons olive oil

FOR THE OKRA
100 g (4 oz) okra
2 tablespoons olive oil

2 lemon grass stalks, chopped
2 lime leaves
2 red chillies, seeded and chopped
1 tablespoon fresh coriander, chopped
1 tablespoon finely chopped onion

FOR THE SAUCE
100 g (4 oz) creamed coconut, grated
150 ml (5 fl oz) milk
1 tablespoon chopped fresh coriander
1 teaspoon cayenne pepper
Salt and freshly ground black pepper

34

Mix together the fish, dill, 40 g (1½ oz) of the flour, egg and seasoning in a bowl. Making sure your hands are well-floured, take handfuls of the mixture and shape into 5 cm (2 inch) patties (it should make 12). Coat each patty with more flour.

Heat the oil in a frying-pan. When hot, fry the cakes for 4–5 minutes each side until golden. Drain on absorbent kitchen paper and keep warm.

Put the okra in a pan of water and bring to the boil. Once the water is boiling, drain the okra and cut them in half lengthways.

Heat the oil in a small frying-pan. Add the spices, reserving half the chilli, the okra and onion. Cook for 4–5 minutes.

For the sauce, melt the coconut in a pan, with the milk and the rest of the chilli. Add the coriander and cayenne pepper and season. Cook on a low heat for 5 minutes, until the coconut has melted; add more water if it seems too thick.

To serve, place the fish cakes in a line along one side of the plate. Put the okra along the other side and pour the sauce over the fish cakes.

READY STEADY COOK Tips
*If you can't buy chopped fish ready-prepared,
mince or process your own from skinned white-fish fillets.*

*Sunflower, vegetable or groundnut oil could be used
as alternatives to olive oil.*

AINSLEY HARRIOTT

SWEET CAROLINE'S CALAMITY MACKEREL

Mackerel with chilli, herbs and lemon, with sautéd sweet potato

Caroline Virgo admitted that she taught herself to cook after leaving home – not just for survival but mainly to impress boyfriends – so Ainsley devised this irresistible and flavourful mackerel dish for her.

SERVES 2	Grated zest and juice of 1 lemon
3 spring onions, to garnish	2 tablespoons finely chopped fresh coriander
1 sprig of fresh coriander	1 tablespoon finely chopped fresh parsley
225 g (8 oz) sweet potato, peeled and sliced lengthways	1 teaspoon finely chopped fresh mint
	1 teaspoon finely chopped fresh basil
4 tablespoons olive oil	1 teaspoon finely chopped fresh tarragon
2 whole mackerel, cleaned and scaled	2 garlic cloves, finely chopped
6 fresh red chillies, 4 seeded and chopped,	½ iceberg lettuce, finely shredded
2 seeded and sliced, to garnish	Salt and freshly ground black pepper

Slit the ends of the spring onions lengthways, without cutting them right through, and put them in iced water until the ends curl. Bring some water to the boil and season with salt. Add the sprig of coriander and the sweet potato and cook for 6–8 minutes, to soften. Remove the sweet potato and pat dry with kitchen paper (discard the coriander). Heat 2 tablespoons of oil in a frying-pan and fry the sweet potato for 2–3 minutes on each side, until browned.

Cut four diagonal slits, 1 cm (½ inch) deep in each side of the mackerel. Put the chopped chilli in a bowl, add the lemon zest and juice, chopped herbs and garlic and season. Mix all the ingredients together and stuff three-quarters into the fish.

Heat 2 tablespoons of oil in a shallow pan. Add the mackerel, cover and cook for 6 minutes, turning halfway through. Then transfer to the grill to brown well on both sides.

Mix the lettuce with the remaining herb mixture.

To serve, heap a bed of lettuce on a plate, add a layer of sweet potato, sit the mackerel on top and pour the cooking juices over. Garnish with the spring onions and sliced chillies.

A I N S L E Y   H A R R I O T T

FIERY-FARING SALMON

Salmon fillet with watercress salad and citrus and sage mushrooms
See photograph

Whilst chopping, Paula Atkins told Ainsley that her favourite pastime is tracing her family tree and taking photographs of gravestones, which astonishes her local photo developer. Paula was delighted with this simple salmon dish.

SERVES 2	2 salmon fillets or steaks
175 g (6 oz) tagliatelle	100 g (4 oz) chestnut mushrooms, thickly sliced
3 tablespoons olive oil	1 tablespoon finely chopped fresh sage
1 onion, finely chopped	2 tablespoons lemon juice or lime juice
75 ml (3 fl oz) white wine	75 g (3 oz) watercress, chopped
150 ml (5 fl oz) double cream	2 red peppers, seeded and thinly sliced
1 teaspoon saffron strands	salt and freshly ground black pepper

Cook the pasta, as instructed on the packet.

Heat a tablespoon of the oil and fry the onion for 4 minutes, until soft. Add the wine and cook for 4 minutes, until the liquid has reduced by a third. Then stir in the cream and cook for 1–2 minutes, until the sauce begins to thicken. Stir in the saffron.

When the pasta is *al dente*, drain it. Pour the sauce over the drained pasta and mix thoroughly. Keep warm.

Brush the salmon steaks with oil, season and cook on a ridged griddle or in a non-stick frying-pan for 7–8 minutes, turning halfway

37

through. Put the mushrooms in a pan with a tablespoon of oil, cover and cook for 2 minutes. Add the sage and half the lemon or lime juice, then cover and cook for another 2–3 minutes, until the mushrooms are soft.

Mix the watercress, peppers, one tablespoon of olive oil and remaining lemon or lime juice together and season.

To serve, arrange the watercress and peppers around the edge of a large serving dish. Using a large carving fork or similar, wind up the tagliatelle and drop into the centre to make nests. Top with the salmon and serve with the mushrooms.

READY STEADY COOK Tip
If you have a griddle pan, make sure it is thoroughly pre-heated before use to prevent the salmon sticking.

A I N S L E Y   H A R R I O T T

A LOAD OF OLD SCALLOPS

Scallops and caramelized shallots, in pastry cases, with potato nests filled with cabbage

On this special Christmas show, *Birds of a Feather* star, Pauline Quirke, admitted that she hated all vegetables except for processed peas, but became a complete convert to cabbage after tasting Ainsley's efforts.

SERVES 2	1 tablespoon demerara sugar
2 medium potatoes	225 g (8 oz) scallops
150 g (5 oz) butter	4 tablespoons white wine
1 egg yolk	150 ml (5 fl oz) double cream
350 g (12 oz) puff pastry	¼ Savoy cabbage, shredded
1 egg, lightly beaten	1 tablespoon soy sauce
1 tablespoon olive oil	1 tablespoon clear honey
8 shallots, 6 left whole, 2 thinly sliced	Salt and freshly ground black pepper

Pre-heat the oven to gas mark 7, 220°C, 425°F. Cut the potatoes into chunks and cook in boiling, salted water for 12–15 minutes until soft. Drain and mash until smooth with 50 g (2 oz) of the butter, the egg yolk and salt and pepper. Put the potato into a piping bag, pipe nest shapes on to a greased baking sheet, and bake for 10 minutes, until golden.

Meanwhile, roll out the pastry and, using a 20 cm (8 inch) plate, cut out four discs. Keep two to one side for the base and then, with a 15 cm (6 inch) plate, take out the centre of two of the discs so you are left with a ring. Discard the centre piece of pastry. Brush the bases with egg and place a ring on top of each base. Brush with more egg. Place on a greased baking sheet and bake until golden and risen.

Heat the olive oil and 25 g (1 oz) of the butter in a pan and fry the whole shallots, until softened and turning golden. Then add the demerara sugar and leave them to caramelize. Meanwhile, in a separate pan, heat 25 g (1 oz) of the butter and cook the sliced shallots, until softened. Then add the scallops and cook for a further 2 minutes, stirring occasionally. Remove the scallops and keep to one side. Pour in the white wine and reduce by half. Then add the double cream and heat through. Before serving, return the scallops to the pan and warm through.

Heat 25 g (1 oz) of butter in a pan and fry the cabbage for 2 minutes. Then add the soy sauce and honey. Stir together well.

To serve, put the scallops into the pastry cases, with the caramelized shallots. Put the cabbage into the potato cases, using a slotted spoon.

READY STEADY COOK Tips
You could buy a 500 g (1¼ lb) packet of ready-to-roll fresh puff pastry and freeze any remainder.

Try to get a mixture of large and small scallops, if possible. The larger scallops will need to be cooked for 1 minute before adding the smaller scallops and cooking for a further minute.

POULTRY AND GAME

R O S S   B U R D E N

POLLO BUCCO

Savoy cabbage 'basket' filled with saffron risotto and chicken kebabs

Animal-mad Joanne Carroll works as a nurse so finds little time for cooking. She has four dogs, including a three-legged dog called Peg Leg, who was rescued from under a bush in Liverpool. Ross cooked up this tasty chicken dish that she can prepare after work.

SERVES 4	5 tablespoons olive oil
1 Savoy cabbage	Juice of 1 lemon
25 g (1 oz) butter	150 g (5 oz) button mushrooms
1 onion, finely chopped	1 large red pepper, seeded and cut
2 chicken stock cubes	into bite-sized pieces
250 ml (9 fl oz) white wine	Finely grated zest of 1 orange
225 g (8 oz) arborio risotto rice	2 tablespoons finely chopped fresh parsley
10–15 saffron strands	3 garlic cloves, crushed
2 skinless, boneless chicken breasts	Salt and freshly ground black pepper

Remove any damaged outer leaves from the cabbage, gently fold back the remaining outer leaves and cut out the middle, so you are left with a cabbage 'basket'. Place the cabbage basket in a pan quarter-filled with boiling water and cook for 10 minutes, until tender. Drain and refresh under cold water.

Meanwhile, melt the butter in a separate pan, add the onion and gently sauté for 3–4 minutes, until soft. Bring 1.2 litres (2 pints) of water to the boil in a separate pan and add the stock cubes and 150 ml (5 fl oz) of wine; keep this stock just simmering. Add the rice to the softened onion and stir to coat in the butter. Pour in two ladles of the hot stock, add the saffron and stir gently. Leave to simmer gently and, when the stock has been absorbed, add a further two ladles of hot stock; stir and leave to simmer again. Continue this process until the rice is tender – about 20 minutes.

Slice the chicken breasts into 2 cm (¾ inch) pieces and put into a bowl with 3 tablespoons of the olive oil and the lemon juice. Stir to coat and set to one side for 5 minutes, to marinate. Heat a griddle pan over a high heat. Thread four kebab skewers with the chicken, mushrooms and pepper pieces and season well. Place the kebabs on the griddle and cook for 2 minutes before turning. Cook for a further 2 minutes and turn again. Repeat this process until the chicken is a rich, golden colour and is cooked. Just before the end of cooking, sprinkle the remaining wine over the chicken, so its flavour is absorbed, and season again.

Shred the uncooked cabbage finely. Heat the remaining 2 tablespoons of olive oil in a wok over a high heat and add the cabbage. Stir-fry until the cabbage has wilted and is cooked.

In a separate bowl, mix together the orange zest, 1 tablespoon of chopped fresh parsley and the crushed garlic.

To serve, place the steamed cabbage basket in a deep serving bowl. Fill the bottom with the shredded cabbage, pile the risotto on top and then add the kebabs. Sprinkle over the orange, parsley and garlic mixture and top with the remaining tablespoon of chopped parsley.

READY STEADY COOK Tip
If you don't have a griddle pan, use a non-stick frying-pan instead.

R O S S   B U R D E N

FEGATINI RUAPEHU

Chicken liver bruschetta with lentil sauce, green beans and fried sage leaves

Ross was more than happy to cook for fellow New Zealander Philip Morris who described his cooking as 'boogie cuisine' – the two most essential ingredients being music and a bottle of wine!

SERVES 2	Large handful of fresh mint leaves
7 tablespoons olive oil	Large handful of fresh flatleaf parsley
4 medium-sized carrots, diced	75 g (3 oz) fine green beans, topped and tailed
3 celery sticks, diced	12 sage leaves
1 shallot, finely chopped	4 slices of white country-style bread
420 g (14 oz) can of green lentils, drained	400 g (14 oz) fresh chicken livers
Juice of ½ lemon	1 tablespoon balsamic vinegar
1 teaspoon ground cumin	Salt and freshly ground black pepper
1 tablespoon chopped fresh mint	

Put 4 tablespoons of oil in a deep frying-pan. Add the carrots, celery and shallot and cook for 5 minutes, until soft, stirring occasionally. Add the lentils, lemon juice, cumin, salt and pepper and mint and mix together. Put the mint leaves and flatleaf parsley in a food processor and process for 30 seconds. Stir into the lentils. Keep to one side.

Bring a pan of water to the boil and blanch the beans for 1–2 minutes. Drain, refresh in cold running water and keep to one side.

In the same pan, heat a tablespoon of olive oil. Fry the sage leaves for 30 seconds. Drain on kitchen paper and keep to one side.

Cut four discs out of the bread for the bruschetta. Heat a griddle pan brushed lightly with a tablespoon of oil and fry the bread on both sides, until golden. Heat a shallow frying-pan with a tablespoon of oil. When hot, fry the chicken livers for 2–3 minutes on each side, until browned. Remove from the pan and keep to one side. Deglaze the pan with the balsamic vinegar. Return the chicken livers to the pan and leave off the heat.

To serve, put a piece of bruschetta on a plate, top with the chicken livers and repeat. Serve the beans and lentils on either side. Garnish with the sage leaves.

ROSS BURDEN

HIT-THE-FLOOR QUAIL

Braised quail with cream sauce, sautéd aubergine and green-bean gratin

Canadian Jane Neisler wanted Ross to create something a little romantic for her boyfriend as the last time she cooked him a candlelit meal, she leant across the table to give him a kiss and set her hair on fire.

SERVES 2
4 tablespoons olive oil
4 quails
100 g (4 oz) green grapes
175 ml (6 fl oz) white wine
1 aubergine, roughly chopped
2 slices of white country-style bread
2 garlic cloves, finely chopped
100 g (4 oz) green beans, topped and tailed
1 small onion, finely chopped
1 teaspoon saffron strands
50 ml (2 fl oz) double cream
420 g (14 oz) can of butter beans, drained
Salt and freshly ground black pepper

FOR THE MAYONNAISE
2 egg yolks
1 tablespoon white-wine vinegar
1 teaspoon saffron strands
1 teaspoon sugar
1 teaspoon French mustard
300 ml (10 fl oz) sunflower oil
Salt and freshly ground black pepper
1 lemon, halved and flesh scooped out, to serve (optional)

Pre-heat the oven to gas mark 6, 200°C, 400°F. Heat a flameproof casserole dish with a tablespoon of oil. Brown the quails all over. Then add the grapes and 75 ml (3 fl oz) of white wine. Cover with a lid and bring to the boil and then reduce the heat to a simmer and cook for 15–20 minutes. Top up the quails during cooking, if necessary.

Meanwhile, put the aubergine pieces in a sieve or colander, sprinkle over a tablespoon of salt and leave to stand, to allow the liquid from the aubergine to drain. This will take about 10 minutes.

In a food processor, process the bread for 30 seconds. Add a tablespoon of oil and a garlic clove. Process again for 20 seconds and set aside. Blanch the beans in boiling water for 2 minutes. Drain and put into an ovenproof dish. Cover with the breadcrumb mixture and cook in the oven for 10–12 minutes until golden and crisp on top.

Heat a tablespoon of olive oil in a pan and fry the onion for 5 minutes, or until softened, stirring occasionally. Add the other garlic clove and fry for a further minute. Season and then add the remaining wine, the saffron and the cream. Bring to the boil, reduce the heat and add the butter beans; then leave to simmer over a gentle heat.

To make the mayonnaise, put all the ingredients, except the oil, in a food processor or bowl and mix together. Then slowly add the sunflower oil, processing continuously until thick and creamy. Season and leave to one side. Heat a tablespoon of oil in a frying-pan and, when it is very hot, fry the aubergine pieces until golden.

Put the quails and grapes on to serving plates and arrange the aubergine around the plates. Pour the cream sauce over the quails. Serve the green beans separately and serve the mayonnaise in 2 scooped-out halves of a lemon or a small dish.

ROSS BURDEN

OSTRICH IN TIME FOR £4.99

Ostrich steak in piquant sauce, potato galettes and stuffed mushrooms

Social worker Sue Riley thought New Zealander Ross was the perfect chef to show her what on earth to do with ostrich. She told Fern that her husband eats absolutely anything, but ostrich was something he'd never tried.

SERVES 2	
1 Savoy cabbage, 6 large outer leaves only	3 flat mushrooms
2 carrots, cut into ribbons	2 red-skinned potatoes, thinly sliced
3½ tablespoons olive oil	100 ml (3½ fl oz) red wine
175 g (6 oz) ostrich steak	Vegetable stock cube
1 onion, finely chopped	1 tablespoon balsamic vinegar
3 slices of white country-style bread	1 teaspoon brown sugar
2 tablespoons chopped fresh tarragon	Salt and freshly ground black pepper
	Sprigs of fresh flatleaf parsley to garnish

Pre-heat the oven to gas mark 6, 200°C, 400°F. Bring a large pan of water to the boil. Blanch the cabbage leaves for 2 minutes and the carrot ribbons for a further minute. Drain and refresh in cold water and set aside. Heat a tablespoon of olive oil in a frying-pan and brown the ostrich steak on all sides. Remove from the pan and wrap the carrot ribbons and then the cabbage leaves around the steak. Secure with cocktail sticks, put on to a baking sheet and bake for 10 minutes. For a well-done steak, cook for 15 minutes.

In the same frying-pan used to fry the ostrich, fry the onion for 3–4 minutes, stirring occasionally. Meanwhile, in a food processor, process the bread for 10 seconds. In a bowl, put the breadcrumbs, tarragon, half the cooked onion and ½ tablespoon of olive oil. Season and mix together. Remove the stalks and put the mushrooms upturned on a baking sheet. Divide the breadcrumb mixture between them. Bake for 8–10 minutes.

Heat the last 2 tablespoons of olive oil in a small pan. Shape the sliced potatoes into galettes, by overlapping them to make two circular discs. Fry on both sides for 2–3 minutes, until golden. Pour the red wine over the remaining onion and add the vegetable stock cube. Stir in the vinegar and the sugar. Season and cook for a further 2–3 minutes, stirring to dissolve the stock cube. Sieve the sauce and keep warm.

To serve, flood the base of a plate with the sauce and put a potato galette in the centre. Cut the ostrich in half, remove the cocktail sticks and place on the potato galette. Serve the stuffed mushrooms separately and garnish both plates with flatleaf parsley.

READY STEADY COOK Tips
Use a potato peeler to cut the carrots into ribbons.

You may wish to use two ostrich steaks and serve one steak per person. The recipe is quite rich and gamey, and one steak halved between two will be delicious, but if you're both feeling extra hungry, opt for one steak each.

Ostrich steak is best served rare, but you can increase the cooking time by five minutes if you prefer well-done meat, although cooking for too long will dry it out.

R O S S   B U R D E N

TACCHINO ALLA SENESE

Turkey steaks with cream and bacon sauce, with watercress
and rice timbales
See photograph

Francesca Parkes met her husband at work. Their eyes met across a crowded room – and what do
they do? They're both opticians! Ross created this visually stunning dish to impress them both.

SERVES 2	100 ml (4 fl oz) white wine
1 chicken stock cube	150 ml (5 fl oz) double cream
175 g (6 oz) long-grain rice	5 black olives, pitted and halved
75 g (3 oz) watercress	Butter
1 tablespoon olive oil	1 beef tomato skinned, seeded and chopped into
2 x 150 g (5 oz) turkey steaks	1 cm (½ inch) pieces
120 g (4½ oz) pancetta, cubed	Salt and freshly ground black pepper
1 onion, finely chopped	

Bring a pan of water to the boil and stir in the stock cube. Add the
rice. Cover and simmer gently for 10–12 minutes or until the rice is
soft. Meanwhile, take the watercress leaves off the stalks and blanch
them in boiling water for 10 seconds. Drain and keep to one side.

Heat the olive oil in a frying-pan and fry the turkey steaks for 5–6
minutes on each side. Fry the pancetta and onion in a dry frying-pan for
5 minutes, stirring occasionally. Then add the white wine and reduce for
20 seconds. Add the cream and boil for a minute. When the turkey is
cooked, put it into the sauce and stir in the olives. Season.

Drain the rice when it is cooked. Put a small piece of butter in the
bottom of two ramekins or cups. Put a layer of watercress on the base
of each. Then half fill with rice, and another layer of watercress and
then fill to the top with rice. Press down firmly.

To serve, turn out the timbales on a plate. Put the turkey steaks on the
plate and pour over the sauce. Garnish with the tomato pieces.

AINSLEY HARRIOTT

TWANGY LITTLE FAT DUCK

Marinated duck slices with mango sauce and minty,
lemony green beans

A fast-food freak, Jane Milner wanted Ainsley to show her how to cook at least one dish in the vain attempt to get herself a husband.

SERVES 2	150 ml (5 fl oz) white wine
2 x 350 g (12 oz) boneless duck breasts	1 mango, peeled, stoned and sliced
3 tablespoons olive oil	5 cardamom pods, bruised
1 tablespoon sesame oil	15 g (½ oz) butter
2 tablespoons soy sauce	1 garlic clove, finely chopped
1 tablespoon clear honey	1 tablespoon chopped fresh mint
2.5 cm (1 inch) piece of fresh root ginger, finely chopped	1 teaspoon grated lemon zest
	Salt and freshly ground black pepper
1 teaspoon dried oregano	Spring onion tassels and sprigs of fresh mint,
5 spring onions, sliced diagonally	to garnish
225 g (8 oz) green beans, trimmed	

Trim half the skin and fat off the duck breast. Cut the duck breast into thin slices and put in a bowl with a tablespoon of olive oil, the sesame oil, soy sauce, honey, ginger, oregano, spring onions and seasoning. Mix together well and set aside, to marinate.

Cook the green beans in a pan of boiling water for 2 minutes. Drain and refresh under cold running water.

Put the wine in a small pan, bring to the boil and simmer for a minute. Add the sliced mango and cardamom pods and simmer for 3 minutes. Remove and discard the cardamom pods. Put the mango sauce in a food processor and whizz until smooth.

Heat a tablespoon of olive oil in a frying-pan, until very hot. Add the strips of duck and the marinade and cook for 4 minutes, until browned, stirring occasionally.

Melt the butter and a tablespoon of olive oil in a pan, add the garlic and cook for a minute. Add the chopped mint, lemon zest and green beans and cook, stirring, for 1–2 minutes.

Pile the green beans on serving plates and top with the strips of duck, using a slotted spoon. Spoon the mango sauce around the edge and garnish with spring onion tassels, sprigs of mint and the scored mango skin (see below), if you like.

READY STEADY COOK Tips

If you like, slice a piece of mango skin with a thin layer of flesh attached, score in a lattice and push the skin up. Reserve for garnish.

Try to buy duck breasts with the skin left on. This adds richness and taste and prevents them from drying out during frying.

A I N S L E Y   H A R R I O T T

MAMMA MIA, WICKED CHICKEN, RICE AND PEAS

Spicy chicken with rice and kidney beans

Italian Sergio Dogliani wanted Ainsley to invent something he could cook for his beautiful wife Emma that was delightful, delicious but NOT ITALIAN!! Although his Italian cooking is excellent, it was getting *basta, basta.*

SERVES 2–3
2 corn-fed chicken leg portions
Juice of ½ lemon
1 chicken stock cube

200 ml (7 fl oz) carton of cocunut cream
2 tablespoons sunflower oil
1 onion, chopped
1 green pepper, sliced

2 tablespoons curry powder
1 tablespoon paprika
2 sprigs of fresh thyme
1 green chilli, seeded and thinly sliced
400 g (14 oz) can of chopped tomatoes

50 g (2 oz) butter
2 garlic cloves, crushed
100 g (4 oz) long-grain rice
200 g (7 oz) can of red kidney beans
Lemon slices, to garnish

Chop the chicken into chunks with a large, sharp knife. Put into a bowl, with the lemon juice, and turn to coat evenly. Rinse the chicken in cold water and pat dry.

In a large measuring jug, dissolve the chicken stock cube in 300 ml (10 fl oz) of boiling water. Add the coconut cream and mix the two together.

Heat the oil in a deep frying-pan, add the onion and most of the green pepper, reserving a little for garnish. Cook to soften and then add the chicken pieces and brown on all sides. Add the curry powder, paprika, 1 sprig of thyme and two-thirds of the chilli, or to taste. Add the tomatoes and 120 ml (4 fl oz) of the coconut-stock mixture and bring to the boil then simmer, stirring occasionally, for 15–20 minutes, until the chicken is cooked through.

Meanwhile, melt the butter in another pan, add the garlic and rice and cook for 1–2 minutes. Add the beans and their juice and the remaining sprig of thyme. Add half the coconut-stock mixture, bring to the boil and cook for 12–15 minutes, until the rice is tender, adding more of the liquid as it is absorbed.

Serve the chicken with the rice and garnish with the reserved pepper slices and lemon slices on the side of the plate. Use the remaining chilli to garnish.

READY STEADY COOK Tip
You could use 200 ml (7 fl oz) of coconut milk if you prefer, or use 55 g (2 oz) of creamed coconut made up to 200 ml with boiling water.

AINSLEY HARRIOTT

IAN'S CHICKEN STUFFETA

Chicken and feta cheese vine-leaf parcels,
with tomato sauce and rice timbales
See photograph

Ian Draper works for a Greek travel company during the summer and admitted that during the
winter he dances in a Greek dance troupe called Marcus and Spencus!

SERVES 2	FOR THE SAUCE
FOR THE VINE-LEAF PARCELS	3 tablespoons olive oil
150 g (5 oz) rice	3 spring onions, sliced
2 chicken breasts, cut into 9 strips	2 garlic cloves, chopped
175 g (6 oz) feta cheese, cubed into 18	6 tomatoes, skinned, seeded and finely sliced
9 preserved vine leaves	3 tablespoons white wine
2 tablespoons olive oil	Salt and freshly ground black pepper
Salt and freshly ground black pepper	6 black stoned olives, sliced, to garnish

Cook the rice according to the instructions on the packet. When
cooked, put the rice into two buttered ramekins or cups.

Wrap a piece of chicken and cube of feta cheese in a vine leaf,
turning in the ends to make a parcel. Season and thread on a skewer
(three stuffed vine leaves per skewer). Fry the vine-leaf parcels in 1
tablespoon of olive oil for 5 minutes; then sprinkle with the remaining
tablespoon of olive oil and finish cooking under a hot grill for a further
15–20 minutes, turning occasionally until the chicken is cooked.

To make the sauce, heat 3 tablespoons of olive oil. Add the spring
onions and garlic and fry for 1 minute. Add the tomatoes and wine,
cover and bring to the boil. Then leave to simmer for 10–12 minutes,
until the sauce has reduced to a fairly thick consistency. Season to taste.

To serve, turn the rice out on to a plate. Spoon the tomato sauce on
to one side of the plate and place the chicken vine leaves on top of
the sauce. Garnish with the olive slices.

READY STEADY COOK Tips

Soak wooden skewers in water for 20 minutes before using,
otherwise they will char. Alternatively, use metal skewers.

Fresh vine leaves should be blanched in boiling water for
3 minutes before use. Vine leaves sold in brine should be drained
and left to soak in boiling water for 20–30 minutes then rinsed
and dried on kitchen paper, to remove saltiness.

A I N S L E Y   H A R R I O T T

CHICKEN AND GREEN POTATO CAKE

Spinach and potato cake with spicy, marinated chicken chunks

Student Mark Tarchetti's plea to Ainsley was to cook him something edible.
The canteen at Durham University is, according to Mark, dreadful and serves mash and
cabbage with everything. Putting together ingredients for less than a fiver was no problem –
he's studying economics.

SERVES 2

2 chicken breasts or quarters, skinned, trimmed
and cut into chunks
1 teaspoon garam masala
½ teaspoon ground turmeric
1 teaspoon ground coriander
½ teaspoon cayenne pepper
1 teaspoon ground ginger
1 tablespoon chopped fresh coriander
Grated zest of ½ lemon

5 tablespoons olive oil
2 large potatoes, very thinly sliced
1 onion, ½ cut into rings, ½ chopped
2 garlic cloves, chopped
1 teaspoon ground cumin
225 g (8 oz) frozen spinach leaves
2 tomatoes, sliced
Salt and freshly ground black pepper
Fresh parsley and lemon wedges, to garnish

Mix together the chicken chunks, garam masala, turmeric, ground coriander, cayenne pepper, ginger, fresh coriander, lemon zest and a tablespoon of olive oil. Ensure that the chicken is completely coated and leave to marinate for 5 minutes (ideally, the chicken should marinate overnight).

Microwave the potato slices on full power for 8 minutes with 5 tablespoons of water. Drain under cold water to separate as they tend to stick together.

Sauté the chopped onions and garlic in a tablespoon of oil for 2–3 minutes, until soft. Add the cumin and the spinach. Season, cover and cook for 3–4 minutes.

Heat a tablespoon of oil and sauté the marinated chicken in a pan for about 10 minutes, stirring occasionally, until the chicken is completely cooked.

Heat 2 tablespoons of olive oil in a frying-pan. Place half the potato slices on the base of the pan, to make a thin layer. Season and then spoon the spinach on top. Place the tomato slices on top of the spinach and cover with the remaining potato slices. Place under a hot grill for 5 minutes, until the potatoes have turned golden brown.

To serve, carefully turn the spinach and potato cake out on to a plate. Spoon the chicken over the top and garnish with the raw onion rings and a little fresh parsley and lemon.

READY STEADY COOK Tip
You could use chicken breasts, instead of chicken quarters, to save trimming and boning.

A I N S L E Y   H A R R I O T T

ON THE GAME, WITH ALAN AND AINS

Wood-pigeon breasts with raspberry sauce, with green beans,
sliced potatoes and avocado with raspberry dressing
See photograph

Alan Cavanagh said he wanted to come on the show so 'I'll have something to bore my children with and, more importantly, have something to talk about from my park bench come my twilight years ... '

SERVES 2
FOR THE AVOCADO WITH RASPBERRY
DRESSING
1 tablespoon red-wine vinegar
3 tablespoons olive oil
Juice of ½ orange
100 g (4 oz) frozen raspberries, thawed
1 avocado
½ orange, peeled and cut into segments
Grated zest of 1 orange
50 g (2 oz) frozen raspberries,
thawed, to decorate

FOR THE PIGEON BREASTS
1 wood pigeon
Grated zest and juice of 1 orange
1 shallot, chopped

1 garlic clove
1 bay leaf
300 ml (10 fl oz) red wine

FOR THE SAUCE
50 g (2 oz) butter
3 shallots, thinly sliced
50 g (2 oz) frozen raspberries, thawed
Salt and freshly ground black pepper

FOR THE VEGETABLES
100 g (4 oz) new potatoes
2 tablespoons olive oil
1 tablespoon sesame oil
100 g (4 oz) green beans, trimmings reserved
Salt and freshly ground black pepper

To make the dressing for the avocado, in a blender or using a whisk, blend the vinegar, oil, orange juice and 100 g (4 oz) of the raspberries. Keep to one side. Cut the avocado in half, remove the stone and peel. Then make a fan by cutting slices 5 mm (¼ inch) from the thin end to the bottom. Fan out on a plate. Arrange the orange segments amongst the avocado slices. Decorate with orange zest and the remaining raspberries and pour over the dressing. Keep to one side.

Remove the breasts from the wood pigeon. Coat the breasts in the orange zest and set aside, to marinate. Put the pigeon bones, shallot, garlic, bay leaf, green bean trimmings, 150 ml (5 fl oz) of the wine and half the orange juice in a large pan. Bring to the boil and then reduce the heat and leave to simmer.

Heat 25 g (1 oz) of the butter in a pan and fry the shallots, until softened. Add the raspberries, remaining wine and 150 ml (5 fl oz) of strained stock. Bring to the boil and leave to reduce by half. Blend with a hand blender then sieve to remove the pips. Season and whisk in the remaining butter, cut in cubes.

Bring a pan of water to the boil and cook the potatoes, until soft. Drain. Toss in a tablespoon of olive oil. Slice thinly and keep warm.

Heat the remaining oil in a pan and fry the wood-pigeon breasts for a minute on each side. Transfer to a baking dish and roast for 6 minutes.

Meanwhile heat the sesame oil in a frying-pan and sauté the beans for 4–5 minutes. Add the remaining orange juice and season to taste.

To serve, put the potato slices and beans in the centre of the plate. Put the pigeon breasts on top and pour the sauce around the plate. Serve with the avocado with raspberry dressing.

READY STEADY COOK Tip
You could serve the avocado with raspberry dressing with crusty bread separately as a starter, if preferred.

FRANK'S DUCK FANCY

Smoked duck breast with lentils, with spicy red cabbage, potato cakes and carrot and orange salad

Fern asked Frank how good his cooking was. 'Just good enough to keep someone alive,' he replied. Ainsley thought this simple duck dish would inspire Frank's cooking to greater heights.

SERVES 2

FOR THE LENTILS
1 tablespoon olive oil
1 onion, chopped
1 garlic clove, chopped
1 teaspoon ground cumin
1 teaspoon ground cinnamon
1 teaspoon paprika
300 g (11 oz) can of Puy lentils, drained
1 tablespoon tomato purée
½ tablespoon chopped fresh rosemary
1 vegetable stock cube
1 smoked duck breast

FOR THE CABBAGE
1 baby red cabbage, shredded
150 ml (5 fl oz) red wine

Pinch of ground cumin

FOR THE POTATO CAKES
2 medium potatoes, coarsely grated
1 tablespoon olive oil
Salt and freshly ground black pepper

FOR THE SALAD
1 tablespoon olive oil
Juice of ½ orange
1 teaspoon poppy seeds
1 tablespoon white-wine vinegar
4 carrots, cut into matchsticks
2 oranges, sliced
Salt and freshly ground black pepper
1 tablespoon chopped fresh coriander

Heat a tablespoon of oil in a pan and fry the onion and garlic, with the cumin, cinnamon and paprika for 3–4 minutes, until soft. Add the lentils, tomato purée, rosemary, stock cube and 2 tablespoons of boiling water. Take the skin off the duck breast and set it aside. Cut half the duck breast into small pieces and stir into the lentils.

In a separate pan, cover the cabbage and red wine and cook gently, with a pinch of cumin, for 12–15 minutes, until the cabbage is soft.

Squeeze the excess liquid out of the potatoes and season. Heat the oil in a pan and form four potato cakes. Fry for 10–12 minutes, turning halfway through cooking, until golden on both sides. Drain on kitchen paper. Put them on a plate and spoon the re-heated lentils and cabbage on top.

Heat the remaining olive oil in a pan. Cut the duck skin into small pieces and fry for 2–3 minutes, until crisp. Drain on kitchen paper.

Meanwhile, mix together the orange juice, poppy seeds and vinegar and season. Arrange the carrot and orange slices on a plate. Cut the other half of the duck into thin strips and put them on top of the carrots. Drizzle over the dressing and garnish with coriander and the crisp duck skin.

ROSS BURDEN

TURKEY TRICOLORE

Poached turkey breasts with cranberry chutney, with orange-topped broccoli and mashed potatoes
See photograph

Pam wanted Ross to create a romantic but low-fat meal to cook for her husband, despite the fact that he is hardly Mr Romantic himself. He proposed to Pam at a football match!

SERVES 2

FOR THE CHUTNEY
1 onion, chopped
225 g (8 oz) cranberries, fresh or frozen, thawed if frozen
100 g (4 oz) soft light brown sugar
½ teaspoon ground cumin
½ teaspoon ground cloves
½ teaspoon ground black pepper
150 ml (5 fl oz) white-wine vinegar

FOR THE TURKEY
175 g (6 oz) turkey breast fillets
300 ml (10 fl oz) rosé wine
6 whole peppercorns
2 bay leaves

FOR THE VEGETABLES
350 g (12 oz) potatoes, peeled and cut in 1 cm (½ inch) cubes
225 g (8 oz) broccoli, cut in two pieces

2 tablespoons low-fat natural yoghurt   Salt and freshly ground black pepper
2 tablespoons chopped fresh basil   Sprigs of fresh basil, to garnish
1 orange

Put the onion, cranberries, sugar, cumin, cloves, pepper and white-wine vinegar in a pan and bring to the boil. Reduce the heat and simmer for 7–8 minutes. Lightly mash with a potato masher and then continue to simmer, until the sauce is syrupy.

Meanwhile, cut horizontally three-quarters of the way through each turkey breast and then open out in a butterfly shape. Put in a large frying-pan with the wine, peppercorns and bay leaves and poach for 10 minutes, until cooked through.

Cook the potatoes in a pan of boiling water for 8 minutes, until tender. Cook the broccoli in a pan of boiling water for 6 minutes. Drain the potatoes and then mash with the yoghurt, chopped basil and seasoning.

Cut a few needleshreds of the orange zest, using a zester. Cut half of the orange into segments and squeeze the juice from the other half. Pile the mashed potatoes on to serving plates and serve with the poached turkey, the broccoli topped with orange segments, needleshreds and juice and the cranberry chutney.

Garnish with fresh basil and the bay leaves.

READY STEADY COOK Tip
Any left-over cranberry chutney can be stored in an airtight container in the fridge for up to a week or in the freezer for up to six months.

MEAT DISHES

BOEREWORS BRAII

Spicy sausage with tomato and mushroom sauce,
game chips andceleriac *rémoulade*
See photograph

Inspired by her South African husband, Sarah Raymond brought along some boerewors spicy sausages. She told us that since having baby Jessica, she's found herself at home spending hours in the kitchen experimenting and has entertained half of Hertfordshire! Ross came up with a new dish for her to impress her guests.

SERVES 2
FOR THE SAUSAGES
350 g (12 oz) boerewors (South African spicy beef sausage) or Cumberland sausage
2 tablespoons olive oil
1 onion, finely chopped
100 g (4 oz) button mushrooms
400 g (14 oz) can of chopped tomatoes
1 tablespoon balsamic vinegar
6 torn fresh basil leaves

FOR THE GAME CHIPS
1 medium-sized sweet potato
Oil, for deep-frying

FOR THE *RÉMOULADE* SALAD
1 egg yolk
1 teaspoon white-wine vinegar
1 teaspoon caster sugar
1 teaspoon Dijon mustard
150 ml (5 fl oz) olive oil
175 g (6 oz) celeriac, peeled and grated
2 tablespoons snipped fresh chives
Salt and freshly ground black pepper

Push two bamboo skewers, in a cross, through the sausage, to hold it in shape. Heat a tablespoon of oil in a griddle pan or frying-pan, add the sausage and cook for 10–15 minutes, turning occasionally, until it's cooked through.

Cook the onion in another tablespoon of oil for 3 minutes. Add the mushrooms and cook for 2 minutes. Stir in the tomatoes, and leave to simmer for 7–8 minutes. Add the vinegar and basil.

Heat the oil for deep-frying to 190°C/375°F or until a cube of day-old bread browns in 30 seconds. Finely slice the sweet potato or cut it into lattice game chips with a mandolin. Deep-fry for 2–3 minutes, until golden and crisp. Drain on absorbent kitchen paper.

Whisk the egg yolk, vinegar, sugar and mustard and season. Whisk in the olive oil very slowly, to make a creamy mayonnaise. Toss the celeriac and chives into the mayonnaise, to make a *rémoulade* salad. Season with salt and pepper.

To serve, spoon the tomato and mushroom sauce on to a serving plate and place the sausage on top. Pile the game chips on top of the sausage. Serve the *rémoulade* salad in a separate bowl.

READY STEADY COOK Tip
Use a food processor to make the mayonnaise. This allows the oil to be added very slowly. If your mayonnaise curdles, start again with 1 egg yolk and add the curdled mixture very, very slowly.

ROSS BURDEN

DOWN-HOME CHOW

Spare ribs with sweetcorn fritters and home-baked beans

Karen Marshall instantly impressed our audience when she told Fern she used to be housekeeper for Wonderwoman (Linda Carter). Karen is, however, very accident-prone and whilst there managed to back Linda's car into a mirror and nearly set her house on fire!

SERVES 2	1 large sprig of fresh rosemary, leaves chopped
FOR THE SPARE RIBS	Tabasco sauce
2 oranges	750 g (1½ lb) pork spare ribs, halved
2 tablespoons clear honey	50 g (2 oz) dried apricots
1 tablespoon balsamic vinegar	Salt and freshly ground black pepper

FOR THE BAKED BEANS
1 red pepper, seeded and sliced into strips
2 tablespoons olive oil
4 tomatoes, chopped
400 g (14 oz) can of soya beans, drained
2 tablespoons tomato purée
1 tablespoon black treacle
Tabasco sauce
Salt and freshly ground black pepper

FOR THE SWEETCORN FRITTERS
1 egg
25 g (1 oz) caster sugar
100 g (4 oz) self-raising flour
100 ml (4 fl oz) milk
50 g (2 oz) shelled pecan nuts, chopped
200 g (7 oz) can of sweetcorn kernels, drained
Salt and freshly ground black pepper
Sprigs of fresh flatleaf parsley and lemon wedges, to garnish

Remove strips of zest from the oranges and put them in a bowl. Squeeze the juice from the oranges and add to the zest, with the honey, the vinegar, rosemary and a few drops of Tabasco sauce; season to taste. Mix well, add the spare ribs and stir to coat the ribs in the marinade. If you have time, leave to marinate in the fridge overnight.

Take the ribs out of the marinade and cook in a moderately hot griddle pan or on a barbecue for 15–20 minutes (25 minutes if you prefer your ribs well-done), turning and brushing with the marinade from time to time.

Meanwhile, put the dried apricots in a bowl, cover with boiling water and set aside to soak.

Cook the red pepper in the olive oil for 2 minutes. Add the tomatoes and seasoning and cook for 2 minutes. Stir in the soya beans, tomato purée, treacle, a few drops of Tabasco sauce and 4 tablespoons of water and leave to simmer for 10–12 minutes, until thickened.

Whisk the egg and sugar and then whisk in the flour and milk, to make a smooth batter. Stir in the pecan nuts and the sweetcorn and season. Heat a lightly oiled griddle or heavy-based frying-pan. Spoon 5 tablespoons of the mixture into the frying-pan or griddle in heaps and flatten slightly. Cook for 5–6 minutes, turning once, until golden.

Drain the dried apricots and scatter them into the griddle pan, with the ribs, and cook for 3 minutes. To serve, spoon the baked beans into a serving bowl and serve with the ribs and sweetcorn fritters. Garnish with flatleaf parsley and lemon wedges.

ROSS BURDEN

KAYLET'S CUTLETS

Lamb filo parcels, tomato sauce and pickled carrot ribbons

'I'm on my second husband,' Kay Penfold told Fern. 'The first hated my cooking, so I need some serious tips to help keep this one!' Ross came to the rescue with this stylish lamb dish.

SERVES 2

FOR THE FILO PARCELS
4 lamb chops, trimmed
4 sheets of filo pastry, cut into 15 cm (6 inch) squares
50 g (2 oz) butter, melted
8 fresh mint leaves

FOR THE TOMATO SAUCE
2 tablespoons olive oil
1 onion, finely chopped
5 tomatoes, roughly chopped
2 tablespoons chopped fresh parsley
Salt and freshly ground black pepper

FOR THE CARROT PICKLE
200 ml (7 fl oz) white-wine vinegar
2 tablespoons caster sugar
1 garlic clove, crushed
6 cloves
4 carrots, sliced into thin ribbons, using a potato peeler
1 tablespoon poppy seeds
Salt and freshly ground black pepper

Pre-heat the oven to gas mark 6, 200°C, 400°F. Heat a char-grill or a frying-pan until very hot. Season the chops and brown on both sides; remove from the heat.

Brush each sheet of filo with melted butter. Place a chop on each filo sheet and add two mint leaves. Wrap the filo around the chop, leaving the bone poking out. Glaze the filo parcels with melted butter. Bake for 10–15 minutes.

Heat the olive oil and fry the onion until soft and translucent.

Add the tomatoes and chopped parsley then season and cook for 8–10 minutes, stirring occasionally, until thickened.

Put the vinegar, sugar, garlic and cloves into a pan and season with salt and pepper. Bring to the boil and leave to simmer until the sugar has completely dissolved. Put the carrot ribbons in a bowl and pour over the spiced vinegar; weigh it down, using a smaller bowl of water as a weight. Leave to pickle for 5 minutes.

To serve, place the chops on a plate and accompany with the tomato sauce. Garnish with the drained carrots, sprinkled with poppy seeds.

R O S S   B U R D E N

PORK DIANE

Pork with celery in cream and mustard sauce, potato galettes, caramelized onions and tomato salad
See photograph

Jazz-lover Diane Thomas decided to bring pork along for Ross, as she'd recently had disasters with lamb and chicken. She'd cooked a chicken leaving a washer inside and a joint of lamb, only to find the next-door dog licking it.

SERVES 2
300 g (10½ oz) whole pork fillet, trimmed

FOR THE CELERY
2 trimmed celery hearts
440 ml (15 fl oz) can of dry cider
150 ml (5 fl oz) double cream
2 teaspoons wholegrain mustard
Salt and freshly ground black pepper

FOR THE ONION MARMALADE
2 tablespoons sunflower oil
1 large onion, thinly sliced
1 tablespoon sugar
2 tablespoons balsamic vinegar

FOR THE POTATO GALETTES
1 large potato, peeled
1 tablespoon sunflower oil
15 g (½ oz) butter

FOR THE TOMATO SALAD
4 tomatoes, skinned, seeded and chopped
2 tablespoons olive oil
6–10 large fresh basil leaves
Salt and freshly ground black pepper
Sprigs of fresh flatleaf parsley, to garnish

Place the celery hearts in a microwavable dish and pour over the cider. Cover with cling film and pierce. Microwave on full power for 10 minutes, or until tender.

To make the onion marmalade, heat the oil in a medium-size pan and sauté the onion. When softened, add the sugar and continue cooking over low heat for 8–10 minutes, to caramelize. Add the vinegar and 2 tablespoons of water, just before serving.

Sear the whole pork fillet in a non-stick pan, to brown it lightly on all sides. Then cook under a medium grill for about 10–15 minutes, turning occasionally, until cooked through and no longer pink in the centre.

Slice the potato fairly thinly with a sharp knife or mandolin. Overlap slices to make two circular cakes 8–10 cm (3–4 inches) across. Heat the oil and butter together in a large frying-pan. With a fish slice, carefully lift the potato galettes into the pan and cook for 4 minutes on both sides, until golden brown.

Put the tomatoes into a small bowl, add the olive oil and season with salt and pepper. Make a pile of 6–10 large basil leaves, roll up tightly and shred them finely. Sprinkle over the tomatoes.

Drain the cider from the celery into a pan and boil it fast over a high heat, to reduce to about 5 tablespoons. Add the cream and mustard and season to taste.

To serve, carve the pork fillet diagonally into thick slices and place on serving plates. Spoon the onion marmalade next to it.

Serve the celery with the cider sauce poured over and then place the potato galettes on the plates, topped with a little tomato relish. Garnish with a little flatleaf parsley.

READY STEADY COOK Tip
You may need to grill the pork fillet for longer, depending on its size and thickness. Take care not to overcook it, though, or it will end up tough!

ROSS BURDEN

STEAK SAVOY

Steaks with cream sauce, stuffed cabbage-leaf rolls
and potato röstis

Pat Dolan confessed that she married her husband Jack because he looked a bit like Barry
Manilow – her great love in life. 'He's got the same long legs and droopy eyes,' she said. Ross
cooked up this special steak for Pat and Jack.

SERVES 2

FOR THE STUFFED CABBAGE LEAVES
4 Savoy cabbage leaves (choose nice-looking, same-sized leaves)
4 mushrooms, finely chopped
7 baby Italian onions or 1 large onion, finely chopped
3 garlic cloves, crushed
25 g (1 oz) butter
Freshly ground black pepper
1 tablespoon chopped fresh rosemary
1 egg, beaten

FOR THE RÖSTIS
2 medium potatoes, grated

50 g (2 oz) butter
Salt and freshly ground black pepper

FOR THE STEAKS
2 fillet steaks
1 tablespoon olive oil
9 tablespoons white wine
4 tablespoons double cream
25 g (1 oz) butter
Salt and freshly ground black pepper

TO GARNISH
1 tomato, skinned, seeded and very finely chopped
10 fresh tarragon leaves, chopped

Remove the spines of the cabbage leaves and blanch them for 1–2
minutes, until they are soft. Refresh the leaves under cold water.

Sauté the mushrooms, six onions (or ¾ of 1 large onion) and two
cloves of garlic in the butter, until soft. Season with pepper and
chopped rosemary. Transfer this mixture to a bowl and stir in the egg.
Put 1–2 spoonfuls of the mixture into each cabbage leaf, roll up the
cabbage leaves to make parcels and steam them for 5 minutes. Put
them seam-side down to cook.

For the röstis, squeeze all the water out of the grated potato, and season. Then heat the butter in a frying-pan. Place a metal ring in the pan and spoon the seasoned, grated potato into the ring. Press down, cook for 2 minutes, and then remove the ring and continue to cook until the potato is golden brown on both sides. Repeat to make a second rösti.

Season the steaks and cook on a griddle, for 4–5 minutes on each side.

To make the sauce, cook the remaining onion and garlic in a tablespoon of olive oil for 3–4 minutes, stirring occasionally, until they are soft. Add the wine and cook for 8 minutes. Stir in the cream and whisk in the butter. Continue to cook for a further 3–4 minutes. Strain the sauce through a fine sieve.

To serve, place the potato rösti on top of the steak and the stuffed cabbage leaves to the side. Surround with the sauce. Garnish with the tomato and chopped tarragon.

ROSS BURDEN

EAST-WEST LAMB

Lamb chops with aubergine fritters, roasted tomatoes and marrow chutney

Johanna came on the show and challenged her mother-in-law, Rita, by daring to claim she was the better cook. Husband Simon just watched nervously from the audience. Ross cooked up this delicious spicy lamb dish, to prove he was the greatest cook of them all!

SERVES 2	2 tablespoons olive oil
FOR THE LAMB CHOPS	2 garlic cloves, crushed
2 x 175 g (6 oz) lamb steaks	Salt and freshly ground black pepper
3 tablespoons olive oil	
2 tablespoons chopped fresh rosemary	**FOR THE MARROW CHUTNEY**
	1 onion, chopped
FOR THE ROAST TOMATOES	225 g (8 oz) marrow, peeled, seeded and
4 tomatoes, sliced	roughly chopped

MEAT DISHES

50 g (2 oz) soft light brown sugar
50 g (2 oz) currants
2 tablespoons white-wine vinegar
1 teaspoon ground cumin
½ teaspoon ground turmeric
Salt and freshly ground black pepper

FOR THE AUBERGINE FRITTERS
1 small aubergine, cut in 1 cm (½ inch) slices
100 g (4 oz) couscous
Grated zest of 1 orange
1 tablespoon chopped fresh sage
Plain flour for coating
2 eggs, beaten
2 tablespoons olive oil
Salt
Sprigs of fresh rosemary, to garnish

Pre-heat the oven to gas mark 6, 200°C, 400°F. Put the slices of aubergine in a colander, sprinkle generously with salt and leave to drain.

Put the lamb, olive oil and rosemary in a bowl. Stir to coat well and set aside to marinate.

Arrange the tomato slices, overlapping slightly, in an ovenproof dish. Drizzle over 2 tablespoons of olive oil and sprinkle over the crushed garlic and salt and pepper. Roast for 10 minutes.

Put the onion, marrow, sugar, currants, vinegar, cumin, turmeric and salt and pepper in a pan. Simmer for 15 minutes, stirring occasionally.

Cook the lamb steaks with a little of the marinade in a frying-pan for 6 minutes, turning once.

Mix the couscous, orange zest and chopped sage. Rinse the aubergine slices and then dip them in the flour, then the beaten eggs and coat with the couscous mixture. Heat 2 tablespoons of oil in a large frying-pan, add the aubergine slices in batches and fry for 4 minutes, turning once, until golden brown. Drain on kitchen paper.

To serve, arrange the lamb steaks on serving plates, with the couscous-coated aubergine, and garnish with sprigs of rosemary.

Serve the roasted tomatoes and marrow chutney separately.

APPLE-BLACK POTATO STACK WITH HONEY-GLAZED PARSNIPS

Stacks of baked apple rings, sautéd potatoes, black pudding and deep-fried onion rings

Anne Ritson from Tyne and Wear told Ainsley that she wished he could be in her kitchen all the time. At home, her husband Alan 'is just constantly in the way'.

SERVES 2

FOR THE APPLE RINGS

2 dessert apples, peeled, cored and sliced in rings
2 teaspoons soft light brown sugar
½ teaspoon ground cinnamon

FOR THE PARSNIPS

2½ tablespoons olive oil
225 g (8 oz) baby parsnips
2 teaspoons clear honey
Juice of ½ lemon
Salt and freshly ground black pepper

FOR THE POTATO, ONION AND BLACK PUDDING

225 g (8 oz) potatoes, cut in 1 cm (½ inch) slices
1 onion, sliced
75 ml (3 fl oz) milk
Oil, for deep-frying
2 tablespoons olive oil
15 g (½ oz) butter
4 tablespoons plain flour, seasoned
275 g (10 oz) black pudding, cut in 2 cm (¾ inch) slices
Salt and freshly ground black pepper
Flatleaf parsley, to garnish

Pre-heat the oven to gas mark 7, 220°C, 425°F. Spread the apple rings on a greased baking tray, sprinkle over the sugar and cinnamon and put under a moderately hot grill for 10–15 minutes, turning once, until golden.

Heat the olive oil in a pan, add the parsnips and cook for 2 minutes. Add the honey and lemon juice and season with salt and pepper. Cover and cook for 3 minutes, turning occasionally. Transfer to a roasting tin and roast in the oven for 10–15 minutes, until crisp.

Cook the potatoes in a pan of boiling water for 4 minutes. Put the sliced onion in a bowl, with the milk, and leave for 5 minutes. Heat the oil for deep-frying to 190°C/375°F or until a cube of day-old bread browns in 30 seconds. Drain the potatoes well. Heat a tablespoon of olive oil and the butter in a frying-pan, add the potatoes, season and sauté for 8–10 minutes, turning once.

Drain the onion rings and coat with seasoned flour. Deep-fry for 2–3 minutes until golden and crisp. Drain on absorbent kitchen paper and keep hot.

Heat the last tablespoon of olive oil in a frying-pan, add the slices of black pudding and fry for 5–6 minutes, turning once.

To serve, layer up the apple rings, potatoes, black pudding and onion rings in the centre of two serving plates. Arrange the glazed parsnips around the edge and garnish with sprigs of flatleaf parsley.

AINSLEY HARRIOTT

BRYN'S 'AM AN' EGGS

Crisp-coated gammon steaks with poached eggs, with tomato sauce

Golf pro Bryn Morris admitted that he'll try anything once and the most unusual thing he'd eaten recently was pigeon. His favourite meal, however, is ham and eggs so he challenged Ainsley to make him a posh version.

SERVES 2	100 ml (3 fl oz) white wine
2 slices of dried bread (dry in the oven,	250 g (9 oz) cherry tomatoes, cut in half
if necessary)	1 tablespoon chopped fresh thyme
1 teaspoon dried mixed herbs	1 tablespoon tomato purée
6 tablespoons olive oil	100 g (4 oz) new potatoes, peeled into
1 onion, finely sliced	'barrel' shapes
1 yellow pepper	175 g (6 oz) sugar-snap peas
3 eggs	Juice of ½ lemon
2 x 200 g (7 oz) gammon steaks	½ tablespoon white-wine vinegar
75 g (3 oz) plain flour	Salt and freshly ground black pepper

Process the bread in a food processor to make breadcrumbs. Put into a glass bowl and add the dried herbs. In a frying-pan, heat 2 tablespoons of olive oil and fry the onion until it's almost caramelized. Blacken the skin of the pepper, by leaving it over a gas flame on the hob or by grilling it under a pre-heated grill for 10–15 minutes, turning occasionally. When completely blackened, put in a plastic bag until cool enough to handle. Take off the skin. Cut in half, seed and slice thinly.

Lightly beat one egg. Dip the gammon steaks into the flour, then the egg and finally the breadcrumbs. Shake off any excess. Leave to one side. When the onions are almost caramelized, add the wine, tomatoes, thyme and the tomato purée. Cook for 3 minutes. Season to taste.

Cook the potatoes and the sugar-snap peas in boiling, salted water. After 2 minutes, remove the sugar-snap peas, allowing the potatoes to continue cooking. Put the peas in a bowl and add a tablespoon of oil and the lemon juice. Season to taste.

Heat 2 tablespoons of olive oil in a frying-pan and fry the gammon steaks for about 5–6 minutes on each side. Bring a shallow pan of water to the boil, with the vinegar. Reduce the heat under the vinegar water and poach the eggs in it for 2–3 minutes, depending on personal preference. Drain the potatoes and toss in the last tablespoon of olive oil. Season to taste.

Garnish the plates with the sliced pepper and peas. Pour on the tomato mixture. Lay the gammon steaks on the plates, with the poached eggs on top. Serve with the potatoes.

READY STEADY COOK Tips
If you are substituting dried herbs for fresh herbs, remember that one teaspoon of dried herbs is equal to one tablespoon of chopped fresh herbs.

Place chopped herbs in small rigid containers, then pack in freezer-proof bags and use straight from the freezer.

FANCY FOOTBALL BIRYANI TEMPURA

Lamb biryani with tempura vegetables and piquant dipping sauce

Referee Eddie McGrath came on in his referee kit and lent his whistle to Fern so she could keep the chefs in tow. A bull once charged on to the pitch when he was refereeing a game. He said, 'The players in the red strip moved the quickest!'

SERVES 4

FOR THE SAUCE
1 orange
2 tablespoons tomato ketchup
1 tablespoon Worcestershire sauce
2 tablespoons honey
Cayenne pepper

FOR THE BIRYANI
3 lamb loin chops or boneless lamb, approximately 300 g (11 oz), cut into 2.5 cm (1 inch) cubes
1 teaspoon ground turmeric
1 teaspoon medium-hot curry powder
1 teaspoon ground cinnamon
1 tablespoon olive oil
1 garlic clove, finely chopped
3 tablespoons finely chopped fresh coriander
1 tablespoon vegetable oil

25 g (1 oz) butter
1 onion
1 red pepper, seeded
1 green pepper, seeded
1 lamb stock cube
200 g (7 oz) long-grain rice
Cayenne pepper
1 tablespoon chopped fresh flatleaf parsley
Salt and freshly ground black pepper

FOR THE TEMPURA
Vegetable oil, for deep-frying
2 egg whites
50 g (2 oz) cornflour
75 g (3 oz) plain flour
120 g (4½ oz) oyster mushrooms
Salt and freshly ground black pepper
1 lemon, cut into wedges, to serve

Grate the zest from the orange and squeeze the juice. Place in a small pan, with the tomato ketchup, Worcestershire sauce, honey and a pinch of cayenne pepper and leave to simmer gently for 10 minutes.

Meanwhile, for the biryani, place the lamb in a bowl and add the turmeric, curry powder, cinnamon, olive oil, garlic and 1 tablespoon of chopped fresh coriander, stirring to coat the lamb. Heat the vegetable oil, with the butter, in a large frying-pan, and sauté the lamb for 5 minutes. Thinly slice half the onion and half the red and green peppers and add to the pan, with the lamb stock cube. Stir to coat the vegetables and add 300 ml (10 fl oz) of hot water, the rice, a pinch of cayenne pepper, 1 tablespoon of fresh coriander and the parsley. Season well. Cover the pan and leave to simmer for 15 minutes, until the liquid is absorbed and the rice is tender, adding more hot water as required.

Meanwhile, for the tempura heat oil for deep-frying, until almost smoking. Place the egg whites in a bowl and add the cornflour, plain flour and enough water to make a thick batter (about 85 ml (3 fl oz)). Whisk for 2 minutes and then season. Thickly slice the other half of the onion, red and green peppers, leaving a few thin slices for decoration. Wipe the mushrooms. Dip the vegetables in the batter in batches and deep-fry at 190°C/375°F for 2–3 minutes, until the batter is golden. Drain on kitchen paper.

To serve, decorate a large plate with the reserved thin slices of vegetables. Place the rice and lamb mixture in the middle of the plate and surround with the deep-fried vegetables. Sprinkle over the remaining chopped coriander and place the lemon wedges to one side. Pour the sauce into a small bowl and serve as a dipping sauce.

READY STEADY COOK Tip
You could use 300 g (11 oz) of boneless lamb, cut into 2.5 cm (1 inch) cubes, instead of loin chops.

LISA'S LAZY LAMB AND LENTIL CURRY

Lamb, lentil and aubergine curry, with little naan breads
and onion wedges
See photograph

Lisa Balbes wanted Ainsley to create something special for her fiancé Paul, who was literally the
boy next door. 'It comes in very handy if we have a row,' she explained,
'as I don't have far to stomp home!'

SERVES 4	1 vegetable stock cube
FOR THE CURRY	1 tablespoon tomato purée
200 g (7 oz) boneless lamb leg steak, cubed	3 tablespoons chopped fresh coriander
2 limes	3 tablespoons olive oil
2 teaspoons curry powder	1 aubergine, cut into 2.5 cm (1 inch) cubes
Cayenne pepper	6 tablespoons crème fraiche
120 g (4½ oz) red lentils, rinsed	
2 tablespoons vegetable oil	**FOR THE NAAN BREADS**
2 garlic cloves, crushed	6 tablespoons plain flour
5 cloves	6 tablespoons vegetable oil
4 cardamom pods	2 tablespoons chopped fresh coriander
2 potatoes, peeled and cut into 1 cm (½ inch) cubes	1 tablespoon tomato purée
1 onion, finely chopped	1 onion, cut into 6, lengthways, with skin left on

Place the lamb in a bowl, with the juice from 1 lime, the curry powder
and a pinch of cayenne pepper. Leave to one side, to marinate for
5 minutes.

Cook the lentils in boiling water until softened, for about 10 minutes.
Meanwhile, heat the vegetable oil in a large pan. Add the garlic,
cloves and cardamom pods and the lamb. Stir-fry over a medium heat

for 5 minutes. Add the potato and onion. Drain the lentils and add to the pan, with the stock cube, tomato purée, 2 tablespoons of chopped coriander and 175 ml (6 fl oz) boiling water, to make a curry consistency. Simmer for 5 minutes.

Heat the olive oil in a frying-pan over a medium heat and add the aubergine cubes. Sauté for 10 minutes, until cooked, stirring occasionally.

For the naan breads, mix the flour and 2 tablespoons of vegetable oil with the chopped coriander, tomato purée and enough water to make a soft dough. Divide the mixture into four and pat each quarter with your hands to make four flat, round patties. Brush the patties and onion wedges with the remaining 4 tablespoons of vegetable oil. Heat a frying-pan over a high heat and place the patties and onion wedges in the dry pan. Fry for 2–3 minutes on either side, until golden.

Add the cooked aubergine to the lamb and lentils, with 4 tablespoons of the crème fraiche and the juice from the second lime. Add a little more water, if it looks too dry. Stir well and heat through.

To serve, place the curry on a large plate and surround with the little naan breads. Pour over the last 2 tablespoons of crème fraiche and garnish with the onion wedges. Sprinkle over a small pinch of cayenne pepper and the remaining chopped coriander.

READY STEADY COOK Tips
To save time, you could use canned lentils, which are already cooked, instead of dried lentils. As a general rule, pulses such as lentils and chick peas double their weight when cooked, so if the recipe calls for 120 g (4½ oz) red lentils, you'll need a 250 g (9 oz) can.

AINSLEY HARRIOTT

FLAMBOYANT FLASH-FLAMING STEAK WITH JAZZY POTATOES

Steaks with green peppercorn and cream sauce,
fried potatoes and orange salad

Trainee nurse Vicky Gambleton chopped very carefully. 'I may be a nurse, but I'm a bit squeamish – I fainted at my first operation!' Ainsley thought she did very well indeed.

SERVES 2
FOR THE STEAKS
450 g (1 lb) new potatoes, scrubbed
1 garlic clove, chopped
2 sprigs of fresh rosemary
3 tablespoons olive oil
15 g (½ oz) butter
2 flash-fry steaks
Salt and freshly ground black pepper

FOR THE SAUCE
2 tablespoons green peppercorns in brine
2 shallots, finely chopped
2 tablespoons white wine
75 ml (3 fl oz) double cream

FOR THE SALAD
½ curly-leaved lettuce
2 oranges, segmented
Juice of ½ orange
½ teaspoon Dijon mustard
1 tablespoon chopped fresh coriander
2 tablespoons olive oil
Salt and freshly ground black pepper

Par-boil the potatoes for 8–10 minutes, until tender. Drain and slice the potatoes fairly thickly and fry them, with the garlic and rosemary, in 2 tablespoons of olive oil and 15 g (½ oz) of butter for 3–4 minutes, until golden brown.

Season the steaks and fry them in a tablespoon of olive oil, for 2–3 minutes on each side. Remove from the pan and keep warm.

For the pepper sauce, using the pan in which the steaks were cooked, fry the green peppercorns and shallots and 1 tablespoon of the juice from the green peppercorns. Add the white wine and cream and cook gently for 2 minutes.

Mix together the lettuce and oranges and arrange in a salad bowl. For the salad dressing, whisk together the orange juice, mustard, coriander and 2 tablespoons of olive oil. Season to taste.

To serve, arrange the steaks on a plate. Surround with the potatoes and pour over the sauce. Serve the salad separately.

AINSLEY HARRIOTT

THE CAJUN GLOUCESTERSHIRE OLD SPOT CHOP

Pork chop with griddled potato wedges,
vegetable fritters and rocket salad
See photograph

'I've brought you some local Gloucestershire Old Spot,' John Parker told Ainsley. 'But I'm a bit worried about being your contestant as, despite being told I'm the world's greatest cook, it was my dog who said it.' Ainsley's dog, Oscar, often tells him the same thing.

SERVES 2
FOR THE CHOP
2 medium-sized potatoes, cut into wedges
2 teaspoons black peppercorns
1 teaspoon ground cumin
1 teaspoon ground ginger
½ teaspoon chilli powder
½ teaspoon paprika
Grated zest of ½ and juice of 1 lime

1 tablespoon olive oil
1 x 750 g (1½ lb) Gloucestershire Old Spot pork chop

FOR THE FRITTERS
150 g (5 oz) runner beans, sliced diagonally
1 large red onion, cut into rings
4 tablespoons milk
2 teaspoons ground cinnamon

300 ml (10 fl oz) vegetable oil	Salt
75 g (3 oz) plain flour	1 bunch of rocket, to serve
1 teaspoon ground allspice	1 tablespoon olive oil
1 teaspoon ground ginger	½ teaspoon paprika

Bring a pan of water to the boil and cook the potato wedges for 10 minutes, until soft. Drain and keep to one side. Meanwhile, put the runner beans and onion rings for the fritters to soak in the milk, add a teaspoon each of cinnamon and salt and keep to one side.

To make the marinade for the pork, crush the peppercorns in a pestle and mortar. Mix in the cumin, 1 teaspoon of ginger, the chilli powder and paprika. Then add the lime zest, half the lime juice and the oil and mix to form a paste. Trim the fat off the pork and remove the bone. Make a few slashes on each side, brush the marinade on both sides and leave to one side while you pre-heat a griddle or non-stick frying-pan. Fry the pork for 5–8 minutes each side. During the last 5 minutes of cooking, fry the potato wedges, turning occasionally, until golden on all sides.

Heat the vegetable oil in a pan. In a bowl, mix together the flour, allspice and remaining teaspoon of cinnamon and season with salt. Drain the onions and beans and dip them in the seasoned flour. Fry in the pan until golden. Drain on kitchen paper and sprinkle over the teaspoon of ground ginger.

Arrange the rocket on a plate. Dress with a tablespoon of olive oil, the remaining lime juice and ½ teaspoon of paprika. Put the deep-fried vegetables in the centre of the plate. Place the pork on top. Arrange the potato wedges around the plate.

READY STEADY COOK Tips
If you can't find a Gloucestershire Old Spot chop, use 2 x 275 g (10 oz) pork chops.

You could deep-fry the onions and beans in a deep-fat fryer at 190°C/375°F for 1–2 minutes until light, crisp and golden.

DESSERTS

DESSERTS

ROSS BURDEN

BUMPY'S BRÛLÉE

Cricket fan Hazel Southgate is known as Bumpy to her mates — it stems from being called Bumpkin as a child. Ross created this delicious brûlée for her to delight all her friends with.

SERVES 4–6

300 ml (10 fl oz) white wine
2 tablespoons caster sugar
6 dessert pears
225 g (8 oz) frozen raspberries, thawed
2 eggs
50 g (2 oz) blanched almonds, finely chopped

50 g (2 oz) self-raising flour
25 g (1 oz) butter
200 g (7 oz) Greek yoghurt
1 tablespoon light muscovado sugar
Fresh basil leaves, shredded
Salt

Put 150 ml (5 fl oz) of water, the wine and 1 tablespoon of caster sugar in a pan and heat gently. Peel and core four pears, add to the pan and poach for 10 minutes.

Put half the raspberries in a pan with the other tablespoon of caster sugar and cook for 3 minutes. Push through a sieve to make a sauce.

Beat the eggs and a pinch of salt together. Mix the almonds and flour in another bowl. Peel and core the two remaining pears and then slice into 1 cm (½ inch) thick rings. Dip in the beaten eggs and coat with the almond mixture. Melt the butter in a frying-pan, add the almond-coated pear rings and cook for 6–8 minutes, turning once, until golden and crisp. Pre-heat the grill to hot.

Lift the poached pears out of the wine, with a slotted spoon. Slice through the pears at 1 cm (½ inch) intervals, leaving the stalk end intact. Fan out the pears and put them in a flameproof dish. Scatter over the rest of the raspberries and spoon over the Greek yoghurt. Sprinkle the brown sugar over the top. Grill for 4 minutes, until the sugar has caramelized (or use a blow torch!).

Pour the raspberry sauce over the pear fritters and sprinkle the shredded basil over the top. Serve with the caramelized poached pears.

SKIP'S GLOOP

The very brave Mat Beardall came on the show to challenge his mother-in-law, Barbara. Both Mat and Barbara are Scout leaders and came on in full uniform to challenge the chefs to make a couple of delicious meals that they could teach the troops! Ross's marshmallow treat will certainly become a campfire favourite.

SERVES 6	2 bananas, thinly sliced
200 g (7 oz) granulated sugar	2 eating apples, cored and sliced
300 ml (10 fl oz) double cream	225 g (8 oz) plain chocolate
200 g (7 oz) marshmallows	25 g (1 oz) butter
1 medium-sized Swiss roll	Icing sugar, to dust
Vanilla essence	Sprigs of fresh mint, to decorate

Put the granulated sugar in a heavy-based pan and just cover with water. Heat gently, until the sugar has dissolved. Boil steadily, without stirring, for 8–10 minutes, until the syrup turns to caramel and is golden brown.

Pour all but 2 tablespoons of the cream into a pan and heat gently. Add all but six of the marshmallows and stir until melted and smooth. Carefully unroll the Swiss roll on a large piece of foil. Sprinkle over a few drops of vanilla essence and a tablespoon of the caramel. Spread half the cream and marshmallow mixture over the Swiss roll and arrange the slices of banana on top. Starting from one long side, roll up the Swiss roll, lifting the foil to help. Wrap the Swiss roll in the foil and chill in the fridge for at least 10 minutes.

Stir the rest of the cream and marshmallow mixture into the caramel. Add the apple slices and simmer for 5 minutes.

Break the chocolate into a pan, add 225 ml (8 fl oz) of water and heat gently, until melted and smooth. Whisk in the reserved 2 tablespoons of double cream and the butter, until melted.

To serve, put the Swiss roll on a deep serving plate and dust with icing sugar. Spoon the apples and caramel-marshmallow sauce on each side. Scatter over the remaining marshmallows and pour the chocolate sauce over the top. Decorate with sprigs of mint.

R O S S   B U R D E N

MY KNEES CRUMBLE

Rhubarb and ginger crumble, with honey and vanilla custard
See photograph

A well-seasoned traveller, Alison Millward told us that the most unusual thing she'd ever eaten was in Peru and that was fried guinea pig! Ross's dessert is slightly more traditional and far more tasty, we think.

SERVES 3	FOR THE CUSTARD
FOR THE CRUMBLE	5 medium egg yolks (size 3)
175 g (6 oz) caster sugar	1 tablespoon honey
450 g (1 lb) bundle of rhubarb (about 6 large	300 ml (10 fl oz) double cream
stalks), cut into 5 mm (¼ inch) chunks	50 g (2 oz) caster sugar
5 whole stem ginger, in syrup,	1 vanilla pod or 1 teaspoon vanilla essence
drained and chopped	75 ml (3 fl oz) milk
175 g (6 oz) plain flour	
75 g (3 oz) butter	
50 g (2 oz) ground almonds	

Pre-heat the oven to gas mark 6, 200°C, 400°F. Put 300 ml (10 fl oz) of water in a pan, add 75 g (3 oz) of caster sugar and bring to the boil. Turn down the heat and poach the rhubarb in the syrup for 4 minutes, until softened. Drain and return to the pan, reserving the syrup. Mix in the ginger and put into an ovenproof dish. Add 2 tablespoons of the syrup.

Rub the flour and butter together in a mixing bowl. Add the almonds and 75 g (3 oz) of the sugar and mix thoroughly, until the mixture resembles breadcrumbs. Spoon the crumble mixture on top of the rhubarb and ginger and bake for 15–20 minutes.

Meanwhile, to make the custard, whisk the egg yolks and honey together, until the mixture turns a pale yellow colour.

Heat the cream and 50 g (2 oz) of caster sugar slowly in a pan. Add the vanilla pod or vanilla essence and milk. When the mixture is nearly boiling, remove from the heat and pour into the egg yolks and honey mixture, whisking vigorously. Return to the heat, stirring constantly, and cook until the custard has thickened enough to coat the back of a wooden spoon. This takes about 20 minutes.

Serve the rhubarb and ginger crumble with the honey and vanilla custard.

READY STEADY COOK Tip
Don't let the custard boil, or it will curdle.

ROSS BURDEN

TARTE TRACIAN

Tracy Dalglish loves puds, but wasn't so hot at making them and asked Ross if he could show her a quick, cheap yet sumptuous dessert to impress her mates at dinner parties. Ross obliged with this lovely fruit tart.

SERVES 2	3 Cox's apples, peeled, cored and
225 g (8 oz) puff pastry	cut into eighths
5 tablespoons caster sugar	450 g (1 lb) frozen summer fruit mix, thawed
75 g (3 oz) butter	3 egg yolks
	300 ml (10 fl oz) milk

Pre-heat the oven to gas mark 9, 240°C, 475°F. Roll out the pastry to make a thin, 18 cm (7 inch) circle. Let the pastry rest in the refrigerator for 10 minutes (or overnight if possible).

Melt 3 tablespoons of the sugar and the butter until the sugar dissolves. Add the apple slices and cook until the mixture thickens and turns golden brown and sticky. Arrange the caramelized apples in an 18 cm (7 inch) round, ovenproof dish and spoon over any extra juice. Lay the pastry over the apples and trim so the pastry fits the dish. Bake for 7–10 minutes, until the pastry has puffed up and turned golden brown.

To make the fruit custard, pass the summer fruits through a sieve, to make a purée. Whisk together the egg yolks and remaining sugar in a bowl. Stir in half of the fruit purée.

Meanwhile, heat the milk almost to boiling point. Pour the hot milk into the egg mixture, stirring continually. Then pour the mixture back into the saucepan and heat very gently until the custard has thickened, whisking all the time. Do not let the custard boil or it will curdle.

To serve, turn the tart out on to a plate; the pastry should be on the bottom. Serve with the fruit custard and remaining fruit purée.

READY STEADY COOK Tips
Use a dish without handles as it will make the tarte easier to turn out.

Don't be tempted to stir the apples while they are in the pan or they will start to break up and not look so attractive when the tart is served. Simply leave them gently bubbling in the sugar and butter until slightly softened and golden.

AINSLEY HARRIOTT

TRIPLE CHOC NUT AND APPLE PANCAKES

Chocolate and apple pancakes, with red wine, curd and cardamom pears

Rosalind McPartlin told us how she had to go ex-directory because she has the same surname as Ant in 'Ant and Dec' and they kept getting phone calls from screaming teenage girls!

SERVES 4

FOR THE PEARS
25 g (1 oz) soft light brown sugar
300 ml (10 fl oz) red wine
6 cardamom pods
2 firm dessert pears, peeled and halved
100 g (4 oz) curd cheese

FOR THE CHOCOLATE NUTS
175 g (6 oz) plain chocolate, broken into pieces
75 g (3 oz) walnut halves

FOR THE PANCAKE BATTER
300 ml (10 fl oz) milk
1 egg
100 g (4 oz) plain flour

Salt
2 tablespoons chocolate icing sugar

FOR THE PANCAKE FILLING
1 orange
25 g (1 oz) butter
1 large cooking apple, peeled, cored and cut in 1 cm (½ in) chunks
2 tablespoons white wine
2 tablespoons caster sugar

TO DECORATE
Icing sugar
Sprigs of fresh mint

For the pears, put the brown sugar, red wine and cardamom pods in a pan. Hollow out the pears slightly with a teaspoon and add the pear halves to the pan. Bring to the boil, reduce the heat and simmer for 15 minutes.

Meanwhile, for the nuts, put the chocolate in a heatproof bowl, place over a pan of hot (not boiling) water and leave until melted. Dip 50 g (2 oz) of the walnuts into the chocolate and put on a plate. Chill in the fridge, to set. Leave the rest of the melted chocolate over the pan of hot water.

For the pancakes, whisk the milk and the egg together. Sift the flour, a pinch of salt and the chocolate icing sugar into a bowl. Gradually beat in the milk and egg, to form a smooth batter.

For the filling, roughly chop the rest of the walnuts and cut a few needleshreds of zest from the orange, using a zester. Melt the butter in a pan, add the apple, white wine, caster sugar, chopped walnuts and orange needleshreds and cook gently for 8 minutes.

Heat a lightly oiled 20 cm (8 inch) frying-pan, add 5 tablespoons of the pancake batter and tilt to coat the base of the pan. Cook for 3–4 minutes, turning once. Repeat to make four pancakes. Keep the pancakes warm. Transfer the apple mixture to a bowl and stir in half of the melted chocolate. Spoon along the centre of the pancakes and roll up.

Slice the orange and cut one slice into quarters. Put the pancakes on a serving plate and scatter over the chocolate-coated nuts. Decorate with twisted slices of orange, drizzle over the rest of the melted chocolate and dust with icing sugar. Put the pears and cooking juices in a serving bowl. Spoon the curd cheese into the pears and decorate with the orange quarters and sprigs of mint.

READY STEADY COOK Tip
If you can't buy the chocolate-flavoured icing sugar, use 2 tablespoons of icing sugar and 1 teaspoon of cocoa powder, instead.

AINSLEY HARRIOTT

DEEP DEVON SUMMER-FRUIT SOUFFLÉ

Fruit soufflé with orange baskets and clotted cream

Janet Till treated all the camera crew by bringing them loads of clotted cream from her home in Newton Abbot, Devon. Not only was Janet able to tuck into an amazing summer pud from Ainsley, but she was seen from every best angle!

SERVES 2	1 lime
2 medium oranges	4 tablespoons clotted cream
3 eggs, separated	4 tablespoons strawberry jam
25 g (1 oz) plus 1 tablespoon caster sugar	Icing sugar, to dust
15 g (½ oz) butter	Sprigs of fresh mint, to decorate
150 ml (5 fl oz) white wine	
225 g (8 oz) summer fruits, e.g. strawberries, raspberries and redcurrants, thawed if frozen	

Place the oranges on a board, with the stalk end of each orange facing upwards. Make a vertical cut on each side of the stalk, one-third of the way through the skin and flesh of the orange. Cut each orange horizontally, in a zig-zag style, and then remove the loose sections, to make a 'basket' with a 'handle'.

Scoop the orange flesh out of the baskets with a teaspoon. Remove the stalk from the handle of each basket and make a small hole in the top of the handle. Push a sprig of mint into the hole.

Put the egg yolks and a tablespoon of sugar in a bowl and whisk for 2 minutes, until pale and creamy. Whisk the egg whites to stiff peaks and then fold into the egg-yolk mixture. Melt the butter in a 23 cm (9 inch) frying-pan. Add the egg mixture and spread evenly over the base of the pan. Cook over a gentle heat for 4–5 minutes, until the underside is golden.

Put the 25 g (1 oz) of sugar and the wine in a pan. Put the summer fruits in a colander over the pan and press down with a saucer to let the juice trickle into the pan. Squeeze in the juice from one of the unused sections of orange. Bring to the boil and simmer for about 3 minutes so that the liquid is reduced by half and becomes syrupy. Fold in the summer fruits and cook for 5 minutes. Cut the lime in half, in a zig-zag style, and scoop out the lime flesh. Pile the clotted cream into the lime shells. Fill the orange baskets with some of the hot summer fruits.

Put the soufflé omelette under a pre-heated grill for 3 minutes until the top is golden. Spread the jam over the omelette and spoon over the rest of the hot summer fruits. Fold the omelette in half and transfer to a serving plate. Dust with icing sugar and mark in a lattice pattern on the top with a hot skewer. Serve the soufflé omelette with the orange baskets and cream-filled lime shells, decorated with a sprig of mint.

A I N S L E Y   H A R R I O T T

ORANGE CHOCOLATE MOUNTAINS

Sweet-toothed Jackie Weaver came along with a bag of her favourite goodies for Ainsley to transform into this wonderful dessert.

SERVES 4	Zest of 2 oranges
175 g (6 oz) plain chocolate	Juice of ½ lemon
5 amaretti biscuits	2 tablespoons chopped hazelnuts
5 tablespoons desiccated coconut	100 g (4 oz) icing sugar
600 ml (1 pint) double cream	10 physalis (Cape gooseberries)
90 ml (3 fl oz) white wine	3 blood oranges, peeled and sliced
75 g (3 oz) caster sugar	Sprigs of fresh mint, to garnish

Break the chocolate into pieces and melt in the microwave on a medium setting, for approximately 3 minutes. Check the chocolate after 2 minutes, to ensure that it does not overcook.

Dip three of the amaretti in the chocolate and then roll them in 3 tablespoons of the desiccated coconut. Set to one side, on baking parchment.

To make the chocolate truffle mousse, whip the cream to soft peaks and then fold in the remaining melted chocolate, with a metal spoon. Then fold in two crushed amaretti biscuits.

For the sauce, mix together the wine, sugar and orange zest and cook for 5 minutes. Stir in the lemon juice, hazelnuts and 2 tablespoons of coconut. Cook for a further 3–4 minutes, until thick and syrupy.

Mix the icing sugar with 3–4 tablespoons of water: the mixture should be of a fairly thick consistency. Dip the physalis into the icing sugar and stand on baking parchment to set.

To serve, arrange the orange slices in the base of a wide bowl. Pipe or spoon the chocolate truffle mousse over the oranges and in the centre. Spoon over the sauce and decorate the dish with the physalis and dipped amaretti biscuits. Garnish with fresh mint leaves.

READY STEADY COOK Tip
The mousse would benefit from being chilled for 2 hours before serving.

VICKY'S CHOCOLATE NUT CRUNCH

See photograph

Vicky Hext admitted to Ainsley that she is a very fussy eater and lives off breakfast cereal and chocolate – and she's getting a little bored with it, so she asked Ainsley to make it a bit more exciting.

SERVES 2	1 x 30 g (1 oz) variety pack of Crunchy
450 g (1 lb) strawberries	Nut Cornflakes
1 tablespoon white wine	150 ml (5 fl oz) double cream
100 g (4 oz) puff pastry	2 kiwi fruit, peeled and sliced
1 egg beaten with ½ tablespoon water	Icing sugar, for dusting
100 g (4 oz) cooking chocolate, at least	Zest and segments of an orange
70 % cocoa solids	

Pre-heat the oven to gas mark 7, 220°C, 425°F. Blend half the strawberries in a blender, with the wine, until smooth. Flour the work surface and roll out the pastry to about 2 mm (⅛ inch) thick. Prick all over with a fork. Using a small saucepan or a 20 cm (8 inch) plate as a template, cut out two discs. Put on two greased baking sheets. Brush both with the beaten egg and bake for 8–10 minutes, until well risen and golden brown.

Melt three-quarters of the chocolate in a double-boiler or bowl set over a saucepan of hot water. Hull and slice the remaining strawberries. Stir the cornflakes into the chocolate and then spread evenly on to baking parchment. Put on a plate and put in the fridge or freezer to cool for 20 minutes. Take the pastry out of the oven and flatten one disc.

Whip the double cream to soft peaks. Spread half the cream on the flattened pastry disc. Lay a third of the sliced strawberries on the cream, with a third of the kiwi slices. Take the chocolate crunch out of the fridge. Peel off the paper, break into pieces and arrange on top of the fruit. Spread the remaining cream on top and then add more kiwi and strawberries. Finally, put the other pastry disc on top. Grate the remaining chocolate over the plate, dust with icing sugar and scatter on the orange zest. Around the edge of the plate decorate with the orange segments and the remaining kiwi and strawberries. Serve the purée separately.

READY STEADY COOK Tips

If you don't already own a zester, make sure you invest in one now. They're cheap, and easy to clean, as well as being quick and efficient to use.

Non-stick baking paper, sometimes called parchment, is great for things containing a high proportion of sugar. But you can lightly grease, then use greaseproof paper if that is all you have. Gaining popularity are fabric reusable 'magic' papers. After use you simply wipe over and they are ready for use again. They also withstand domestic oven temperatures.

INDEX

A

apples
  caramelized apple rings 17-18
aubergines
  deep-fried slices with feta filling
    15-16
  fritters 68-9
  sautéd 44-5
avocado with raspberry dressing 55-6

B

black pudding apple potato stack 70-1
broccoli
  orange topped 58-9
brûlée, Bumpy's 81
bruschetta pesce 26-7

C

cabbage
  savoy 'basket' filled with saffron
    risotto 41-2
  spicy red 57-8
  stuffed leaf rolls 67-8
carrots
  pickled ribbons 64-5
  ribbons 29-30
celeriac *rémoulade* 61-2
cheese
  chicken and feta cheese vine-leaf
    parcels 52
  deep-fried aubergine slices with

feta filling 15-16
  mushroom and cheese risotto 18-19
chestnut pastries with stuffed
  mushrooms and celery sauce
  10-11
chicken
  kebabs 41-2
  liver bruschetta with lentil sauce 43-4
  spicy marinated chunks 53-4
  spicy with rice and kidney beans
    50-1
  and feta cheese vine-leaf parcels 52
chocolate and apple pancakes 86-7
chocolate nut crunch 91-2
clams with spaghetti and tomato soup 28
courgettes
  ribbons 24-5
cranberry chutney 58-9
crumble, rhubarb and ginger 83-4
curry
  lamb biryani 73-4
  lamb, lentil and aubergine 75-6
  vegetable served in a pumpkin 17-18
custard
  honey and vanilla 83-4
  fruit 84-5

D

duck
  marinated slices with mango
    sauce 49-50
  smoked breast with lentils 57-8